WAR MACHINES
LAND

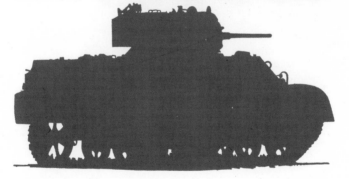

WAR MACHINES
LAND

Edited by Simon Ransford

OCTOPUS
Octopus Books

Introduction

This book tells the story of the greatest, most celebrated and most formidable land-based war machines. Formidable, that is, within their own era.

By the definition used in this book a stone in a sling — or a simple spear — can be a devastating weapon of war. A war machine can be a device, a contraption, a complicated mass of modern electronic equipment. It can even be a theory of attack or defence. It can, for example, be the formation adopted by the Swiss pikemen or the Roman phalanx in which the Roman shields formed a 'platform' with, in relative terms, something of the fire-power resistance of the armour of a tank.

Throughout history there are certain obvious breakthrough points in which superior technology gave one or other nation or civilization the edge in warfare. This book is a selection of these points and memorable phases of development. It is, therefore, in a sense a pictorial catalogue of principal land-based weapons and the theories of weaponry.

This book — with its companion volumes on sea and air war machines — is a brilliant visual guide which helps the reader to build up a 'time-scale' picture of the ebb and flow of civilizations and of the gradual growth over the centuries of that background technology which now dominates our lives — a technology which has invariably found impetus in the quest for military mastery. For it is true to say that throughout history war machines have reflected the scientific capacities of their period.

A Sherman tank covers troops near Anzio in 1944

Contents

First published in 1975 by
Octopus Books Limited
59 Grosvenor Street
London W1 under licence
from Lynx Press Ltd.
601 Union House
Hong Kong

Created and devised by
Berkeley Publishers Ltd

ISBN 0 7064 0416 5

© 1975 Lynx Press Ltd.

Distributed in USA by
Crescent Books
a division of Crown
Publishers Inc. 419 Park
Avenue South, New York
NY 10016

Printed in Hong Kong

WAR ON THE LAND

THE FIRST DEVICES OF WAR
Sticks and Stones

The earliest devices used by man for hunting and fighting were primitive extensions of his own physical strength. In one form or another, sometimes in a simple device, sometimes in a more sophisticated one, man has continued to try to extend his power through an increasingly complex range of contraptions.

In the beginning man stood naked, with only his fists with which to grip, strike, tear and strangle his enemy. When he held a stone in his hand, he discovered that he could strike with greater force and inflict a deeper wound. When he wielded a stick, the length of his arm was doubled and the weight of his blow vastly increased. When he learnt to throw both stick and stone, the range of his firepower was extended far beyond the threatening reach of club or knife or axe. Bullets and rockets are the sticks and stones of today.

In ten thousand years of inventive destruction, between the hurled stone and the guided missile, man has produced an astonishing array of war devices. Not all of these have been wholly offensive. In defence, man has had to strengthen his own skin, first with the skin of other animals, later with metal, sometimes with massive walls, fortifications and extensive barriers. More often than not, the ideal war machine has incorporated the functions both of defence and attack. The armed footsoldier with his shield was as much a machine of war as the armoured horse, the elephant or the tank. To think only of mechanical devices as the true war machines would be to pass over those devices which, though primitive by comparison and less complicated in structure, nonetheless dominated the battlefields of many parts of the world for thousands of years.

From Stone to Bronze

The wooden stick became a spear with a sharpened point; the tip of the spear was sometimes shaped in the fire, which gave it a greater capacity for penetration. Then the stone and the stick were combined to form the axe and a still sharper spear.

Flint was first used almost 10,000 years before Christ. Its excellent cutting properties and its ease of access, on or near the surface of the earth, made it the ideal material for man's most elementary weapons. It is probable that flint came into use quite independently both in Africa and China.

Flint was, however, impractical for daggers and swords because it broke easily. Early axes and daggers were sometimes made of copper, which the Egyptians also used for spears at least 3,000 years before Christ. Copper alone proved far too soft and required constant sharpening, so tin was added as an alloy to form bronze.

Bronze was used by the Shang Dynasty in China in 1800 B.C. for spears, swords, axes and daggers. One particularly effective device called a 'ko', consisted of a dagger fixed to an axe handle. A great many bronze-age weapons have also been found in graves and barrows in Scandinavia, dating from 1,000 years before Christ. The Scandinavian axe was called a 'palgrave'.

Another metal used effectively in similar weapons was iron, which was probably first smelted in Asia Minor in about 3000 B.C. The Assyrians made good use of iron-tipped weapons when they ousted the Sumerians from the area between the Tigris and the Euphrates rivers. The Hittites, who swept through Asia Minor in the middle of the Second Millenium B.C., also used iron weapons with marked success.

Slings and Bows

It is one step forward to grasp a weapon in the hand, another to throw it, but the effect becomes greater when further impetus is provided by such devices as the sling and the bow.

The sling has been used since earliest times. In

Above: Assyrian archers and slingers advance behind a heavy shield.
Right: Bronze dagger and arrowheads, once used by Greek warriors.
Below: Acheulean hand axes from prehistory.

its simplest form it was a strip of leather folded over so that the thrower held the two ends and the stone was contained in the loop. The sling was then swung round in the hand several times to gain momentum until at the right moment one end of the leather strip was released and the stone hurled out. It was effective as a lethal weapon up to a distance of about 25 yards.

Once again, it was the Assyrians who recognized the value of the sling; although normally it was considered a weapon for individual combat, they used it effectively in their organized armies. The best sling-stones were usually to be found in river beds. The Assyrians occasionally exacted a supply of these stones as tribute from subjugated tribes in Asia Minor.

One of the most famous incidents in which the sling proved its worth was in the single-handed combat between the Israelite David and the Philistine Goliath, set against each other to decide the outcome of the general battle in front of their respective armies. The giant Goliath, protected by armour and wielding a sword, and possibly a spear as well, proved no match for the sling-stone of young David, which struck him between the eyes and knocked him down.

A sophisticated type of sling held the stone in a special patch that was attached to a couple of thongs. A more effective development, although difficult to use accurately, was a sling attached to the end of a long pole. The momentum attained by the sweeping arc of the pole gave the stone great additional power and range.

The combination of bow and arrow was the next most important war device to develop. As with swords and spears, the earliest arrows were tipped with stone; later they were fitted with iron and bronze. Examples of the first bows can be seen in Neolithic cave paintings in Spain.

The Sumerians did not use the bow, but the Assyrians came with archers not only on foot but also mounted on horses and in chariots. The Assyrians generally used a long arced bow, whereas the Egyptians, who had dominated the Nile delta ever since the Sumerian Empire had begun, used as well as the single arced bow a double curved bow, consisting of two pieces of wood bound together or joined by a handgrip made of horn.

Blow-pipes and Spear-sticks
Both the sling and the bow were part of the equipment of civilized nations and organized armies. The sling developed into a more elaborate device, the ballista or missile-throwing machine of the Assyrians and Romans, and the bow made its most effective re-appearance as the longbow of the English army in the 14th Century. Two other devices, as primitive as the sling, failed to survive in organized war. These were the blow-pipe and the spear-stick.

The blow-pipe is still used in certain parts of Africa and by primitive tribes in the Amazon jungle and New Guinea. With or without a poison

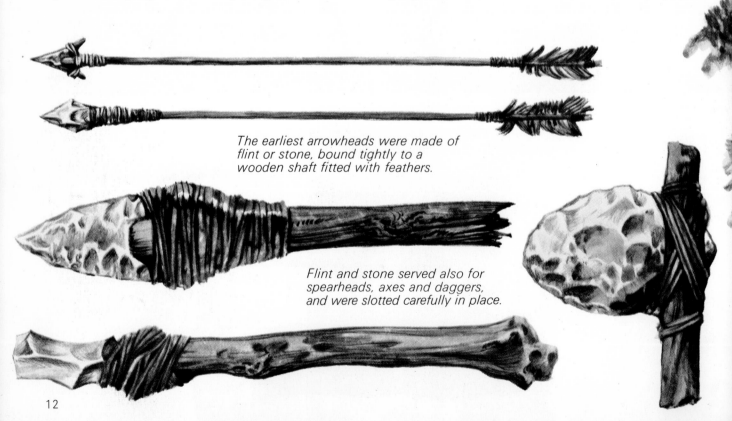

The earliest arrowheads were made of flint or stone, bound tightly to a wooden shaft fitted with feathers.

Flint and stone served also for spearheads, axes and daggers, and were slotted carefully in place.

dart, it is a simple and effective weapon with a range that enables it to be used against an unsuspecting enemy.

The spear-stick had the same advantage as the sling attached to a pole. The base of the spear fitted into a notch in the stick along which the spear lay. The thrower held the stick and used it as a lever to give added impetus to the spear itself.

Protection for the Soldier

There was little point in arming a soldier with an offensive device unless he survived to use it and was therefore given some protection. Armour gradually became an increasingly important part of the foot-soldier's equipment. The oldest surviving illustration of armed warriors – the Standard of Ur, which dates from 3500 B.C. – shows soldiers with clubs and spears wearing leather protection. We know that the Sumerians used a metal-studded leather cape and a leather and metal helmet.

The Egyptians at first used only a shield for protection. This was made of animal skins fitted over a wooden frame; later the shields were completed with a metal rim. By 1250 B.C., the Egyptians wore breastplates made from pieces of leather or crocodile skin, or small metal plates.

The Assyrians were particularly careful to use armour. Even their horses – highly valued assets, well worth protection – were covered in cloths made probably of wool overlaid with flaps of leather and, occasionally, pieces of metal.

Stone Age man was well equipped with bows and arrows, knives, spears and axes, sharpened by laboriously rubbing stones together until a point was achieved.

Armed with such weapons, man became first a hunter then a warrior.

13

THE WAR CHARIOT
Solid and Cumbersome

It would seem a simple step to fit the horse with some kind of platform on which the soldier could stand and from which he could more easily use his weapon. But a certain amount of mystery surrounds the origin of the chariot. We do know, however, that chariots were an important war machine in Mesopotamia as long ago as 3000 B.C. and we can guess that they probably date from even earlier.

These first recorded chariots were primitive affairs by comparison with the later models known to the Romans. The wheels were solid and cumbersome. The bodywork had a stout wooden frame over which skins were stretched to give protection to the driver and his companion, usually a spearman or javelin thrower.

Even in these very early days there seem to have been two distinct types of chariots – two-wheeled and four-wheeled varieties. Chariots found in Egyptian royal tombs have high protective shields guarding the riders. From this we can deduce that the chariot was used as a first-strike weapon, designed to smash an enemy line by the thrust and terror of the initial attack. A line of several thousand war chariots must have presented a formidable spectacle. Once a line or an enemy position had been broken up, the charioteers leaped down into the fray to fight as foot-soldiers.

Speed and the Spoked Wheel

By about 2500 B.C. considerable refinements had taken place in chariot design. Greater speed was achieved through the introduction of spoked wheels, which considerably lightened the chariot. The effectiveness of the pulling pole was also improved by arching the pole over the backs of the horses. This enabled greater manoeuvrability. But in one curious respect the chariot remained unchanged for thousands of years: the harnessing of the horses was never efficient. The wide leather collars of the yoke attached to the pole were slipped round the horse's neck and not its chest. In consequence the true pulling potential of the horse was never fully exploited and the war chariot never reached its maximum speed capacity.

The early Egyptians adopted the chariot from a rival tribe called the Hyksos and were responsible for many of the refinements in its development.

The first recorded battle in which the clever use of chariots won the day was Ramses II's

victory over the Hittites about 1290 B.C., at Kadesh, in Syria. The light Egyptian vehicles – so light that it is difficult to see how they could have survived tough usage over rough ground – armed with long-range bows, proved decisive against the heavier Hittite chariots, which were only armed with short-range spears.

The Spread of the Chariot

By the end of the Second Millenium B.C. the four-

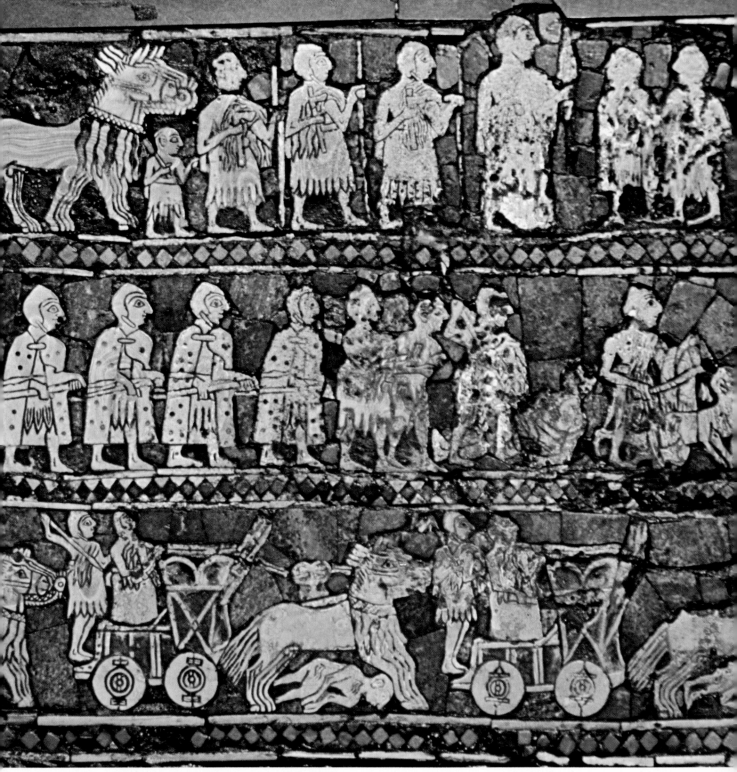

Heavy wooden chariots and the first recorded army from the Sumerian Standard of Ur, 2750 B.C.

wheeled war chariot in its more sophisticated Egyptian form was in use throughout the eastern Mediterranean countries. By that time, also, the chariot had been introduced to the powerful and highly developed Minoan culture centred in Crete and was a favoured war machine throughout the southern European mainland. By the 14th Century B.C. the Chinese were using chariots not unlike the Celtic chariots of the two-wheeled variety that were constructed in Western Europe.

Chariots were in common military (and civilian) use in central and northern Europe by about 1000 B.C. and the Celtic tribes introduced them into Britain in about 500 B.C. These Celtic chariots were heavier in design than the late Egyptian and Greek chariots. Metal was used for the axles and pole and the wheels themselves were often fashioned in solid metal. The Celtic people frequently adorned their chariots with finely worked enamel inlays.

15

THE EARLIEST SIEGE MACHINES
The Assyrian Assault Tower

With the appearance of fortified cities and organized armies in Asia Minor, siege machines became increasingly important. Just as they had led the way in so many other military fields, it was the Assyrians who first laid proper emphasis on cohesive army organization and an effective siege train well equipped.

The land between the Tigris and the Euphrates was largely without natural defences – a flat, open and vulnerable area. For self-protection, the Assyrians had to build substantial forts. Their understanding of the techniques involved naturally helped them to appreciate what was needed to attack forts as well as to defend them.

The most formidable siege machine that they developed was the mobile battering ram, which was often combined, within the same machine, with a double assault tower. The tower was built of wood and wickerwork. It was drawn up on wheels to the walls of the besieged fort and, while the heavy-ended ram, looking remarkably like a modern tank gun, thudded against gate or wall, archers and spearmen fired a withering volley at the defenders along the parapet. The tower could also be used as an assault platform once it had been brought close up against the fortification.

Other hand-propelled armoured vehicles, made of similar materials, were used to protect troops attempting to get close to the walls in order to scale them with ladders or to follow up any breach that had been prepared by the battering ram. The Assyrians were also pioneers in the art of undermining the walls of fortifications: armoured vehicles could be used for protecting the 'sappers', as they were called.

The Torsion Catapult of the Macedonians

It was the tyrant Dionysus I of Syracuse who may well first have discovered and employed catapult artillery. This was in about 400 B.C. Though used to excellent purpose throughout his campaigns, the catapult was not fully developed until Philip of Macedon recognized its potential as a military machine more than 60 years later.

Philip's engineers invented the torsion catapult. The base end of a long arm was fixed to a spring consisting of tightly twisted rope. The extended end of the arm was winched down against the force of the spring and a hollowed out bowl or a sling at the end of the arm was fitted with the missile. When the arm was released it shot upright and was brought to an abrupt vertical stop against a solid cross-bar. The missile – stone or burning material – continued through the air to land, causing havoc among the defenders. By angling the whole machine or changing the angle of the cross-bar, the trajectory of the missile could be altered.

Philip used these machines at the sieges of Perinthes and Byzantium. It is not hard to imagine the consternation that such a barrage of firepower would have had on a civilian population and also on the morale of the besieged warriors, quite apart from the physical effect of large boulders crashing against the walls, through the roofs of houses, or ploughing into groups of defenders.

Philip's son, Alexander the Great, continued the siege tactics of his father and gave further impetus to siegecraft by instituting a corps of engineers whose special responsibility it was to develop effective siege machines. In his long, penetrating campaigns east toward India and the River Sutlej, Alexander used this corps of engineers to construct siege weapons when and where they were needed out of materials available on the site. This was a good deal easier than dragging the ungainly machines across the thousands of miles of unknown country that his armies had to traverse.

Above: A bust of Alexander from the Ottoman Museum.
Right: An Assyrian army attacking a well-defended fort with archers and a moving siege tower and battering ram, from a bas-relief found at Nimrod.

Above: Alexander the Great, riding on the left, was a master of land warfare.

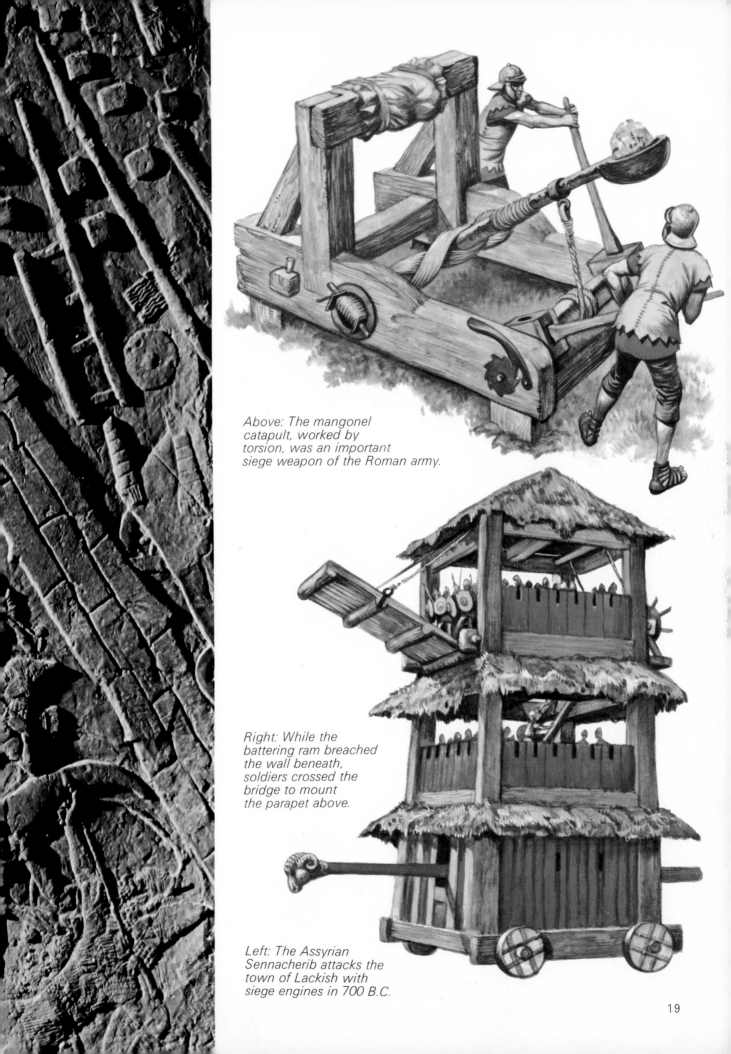

Above: The mangonel catapult, worked by torsion, was an important siege weapon of the Roman army.

Right: While the battering ram breached the wall beneath, soldiers crossed the bridge to mount the parapet above.

Left: The Assyrian Sennacherib attacks the town of Lackish with siege engines in 700 B.C.

19

FRONTIERS AGAINST INVASION
The Great Wall of China

The natural development of the walled city was a system of defence that halted the enemy even before they entered the homeland, before they could attack either with massed troops or with artillery the cities and forts within the homeland. The Great Wall of China was just such a device. It dates from 300 B.C. and has been described as the greatest feat of military engineering in history.

Before the emperor Shih Huang Ti established China along the lines of the country we know today, it consisted of a number of walled-in territories. Shih, the first Emperor of a united China, knocked the walls down and constructed the Great Wall as a formidable obstacle to his enemies, the nomads to the north.

The wall stretched for about 1,600 miles, from the Yellow Sea to Central Asia. The entire length of this enormous barrier against the warlike Huns to the north was heavily fortified, with towers placed at strategic intervals about 200 yards apart.

These 40-feet-high towers topped a wall that in its steepest place was at least 30 feet high. The wall itself was built mainly of earth and stone, faced with bricks. Great modifications took place over the centuries and in the 15th and 16th Centuries the central sections were rebuilt and strengthened. A roadway along the top of the wall was designed to take a column of marching soldiers, and chariots could also run along its length, covering the wall from end to end.

On the Edge of the Roman Empire

A smaller and later version of the Great Wall was built in Britain by the Roman Emperor Hadrian. Hadrian's Wall was constructed between 117 and 138 A.D. and marked the northernmost limit of the Roman Empire. It also helped to keep at bay the warlike tribes of Picts that raided the north of England and terrorized the populations of the cities and the countryside.

The wall stretched for 73 miles across the narrowest part of Britain, from Wallsend, on the river Tyne, to Bowness, on the river Solway. It was defended by a system of forts, mile-castles and fortified turrets. In all, Hadrian's Wall boasted more than 80 mile-castles, between which the turrets were built for added protection. The main wall was an average of 15 feet high with a six feet parapet on top. The Roman forts were quite sophisticated affairs with central heating and hot bath facilities laid on.

Hadrian's Wall was permanently manned by cohorts of conscripted soldiers, both infantry and cavalry, and a Roman legion at nearby York was always on hand in case of any serious trouble from the north.

In comparison with China's vast creation, Britain's wall was very small, but it was nonetheless an impressive piece of war machinery.

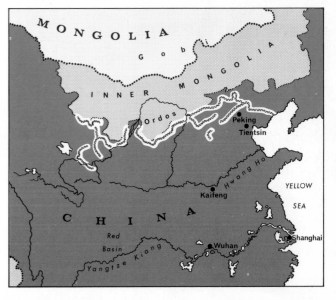

Above: The map shows the extent of the Great Wall of China.
Right: Running through such mountainous regions, the wall is a great feat of engineering.

Left: Hadrian's Wall made use of natural defences as well. This photograph is looking east.

THE GREEK PHALANX
The Hoplites – an Elite Force

Once some sort of organization had been introduced into the warring armies of Asia Minor, the foot-soldier became of greater importance, not as an individual but as an integral part of a military formation. In the earliest days of the Assyrian empire dense concentrations of foot-soldiers had been employed but had been displaced in favour of the greater manoeuvrability of light cavalry. It was therefore in Greece, where the mountainous and broken terrain did not suit cavalry nearly so well as the plains of the Euphrates, that the foot-soldier in formation – the phalanx – was first established with any marked success.

Whereas military power in Greece had been with the nobility in their chariots, internal reasons in about 600 B.C. hastened the transference of this power to the middle class citizens. Organized into infantry, they were called the hoplites. Above all else, these were the people, led by the Spartans, who established the dominance of the Greek city states in the eastern Mediterranean.

The hoplites were the élite among the Greek warriors and since their equipment was not by any means cheap it was something of a privilege to belong to the class from which they were picked. They were very conscious of this honour.

Armour consisted of the famous round shield, held in the left arm by an arm loop and a hand grip. In the use of the shield lay the essence of the formation. Each soldier held his shield so that it overlapped his neighbour, thus protecting half of himself and half of the man on his left. This resulted in a serried wall of shields interrupted by the eight-feet-long spears that each hoplite held in his right hand in the initial stages of the battle. Sometimes this spear was pointed at both ends so that if one point broke the spear could be reversed. For closer fighting the hoplite had a short stabbing sword held from a strap under his left arm.

Apart from his shield, which was usually decorated with the owner's motif and often embossed with some kind of animal's head (this provided a means of crushing his opponent in close combat), the hoplite was protected by shin guards, called greaves, and back and breast plates. The more elaborate and best known of these were close-fitted and fashioned with simulated muscles raised from the surface. Helmets varied in style, with emphasis laid on cheek guards and nose guards, The early Corinthian

helmet, hammered out of a single piece of bronze, was all-enveloping. The Doric helmet was more elaborate and had a large horsehair crest.

Marathon and Thermopylae

Initially the hoplite formations were used in the internal wars between the Greek states themselves. Victory in these conflicts depended largely on numbers. It was not until the phalanx came up against enemies from outside Greece that it was able to prove itself to be an irresistible machine of war.

The Persians invaded Europe in 490 B.C. with a highly efficient élite army, whose pride were the lightly armed archers. They landed in the Bay of Marathon, north-east of Athens. 11,000 Athenians faced 15,000 Persians and employed the regular tactics of the phalanx to put them to

rout. One of the most important factors in the success of the phalanx was that, though well-armoured, the hoplites were not too encumbered to advance quickly. They formed a highly mobile force that could be adapted to conditions.

This agility was used to close with the enemy before the Persian archery took its full toll. Then, holding the centre just long enough to envelop the Persian flanks, the Athenians attacked the enemy where they lacked protection and drove them back to the sea. Over 6,000 Persians fell and barely 200 hoplites.

Ten years later, at Thermopylae, 300 Spartan hoplites held off an overwhelming superior force of Persians for three days. The battle at the narrow pass has become one of history's most renowned encounters. Persian cavalry, reputed to be the best in the world, and Persian open

Hoplites advancing in line, part of a frieze from the monument of the Nereids. When fighting, each shield would overlap the hoplite to the left.

infantry were no match for the Greek phalanx.

It was only when Philip of Macedon combined the use of the phalanx in the centre with heavy cavalry on the wings and a force of light pursuit cavalry that the Greeks were defeated. This was at the Battle of Chaeronea, in 338 B.C.

Philip subsequently developed the phalanx, increasing its breadth and depth to 16 ranks of 96 men each, and lengthening the spear (*sarissa*), to as much as 12–15 feet, or more. Lengths varied so that the phalanx presented a formidable and fearful wall of spear-points. With this machine Philip and his son, Alexander, went on to many further victories.

23

THE LEGIONS OF ROME
A Formidable Fighting Machine

The Greeks were not the only ones to organize an effective fighting machine out of their infantry. The organization of the Roman army was partly learned from its former enemies, the Etruscans. On the whole, new ideas are evolved by a process of adaptation; complete innovation is rare. As a result of a series of defeats and setbacks at the very close of the 2nd Century B.C., the Roman army was reorganized with such success that it became the most formidable military force the world had ever seen.

The Roman legion in the 1st Century B.C. consisted of 4,000–5,000 men. These were divided into 10 *cohorts* of approximately 400–500 men each, and each cohort was subdivided into six *centuries*. It is clear that each century did not necessarily contain 100 men; its full complement would rarely be realized, but it served as a useful basic unit whose numbers varied depending on the situation, recruitment, illness, depletion by death, and so on. Nor was the Roman legion a standard formation throughout the hundreds of years of its existence. By A.D. 400 its organization and equipment had changed greatly – the usual strength of an effective legion unit was then 1,000 men though it was often less.

The centurion was the lynch-pin of the entire organization, invaluable to his commanders as much as to his soldiers because of the depth of his combat experience. It was often the centurion who was responsible for turning a crisis into victory, despite the orders of his superiors.

Within the cohort, the centuries were organized into two ranks of three centuries each, the second rank to support the first. Within the legion, the cohorts were drawn up in three rows. Formation on this basic plan differed. The simplest was to have four cohorts in the front, with three behind to follow through in the gaps between the first four. The third row of three cohorts was then used as a reserve in case the engagement was prolonged and the first cohorts needed relief; in retreat, the third line acted as cover for its companions.

An alternative formation set three cohorts in the front line, three in the second and four to the rear. But the tactics employed were much the same. Flexibility, support, leap-frogging one line of cohorts through another, acting as cover, formations in columns, in squares, in line abreast – all these manoeuvres were easily undertaken once the basic units had been established. This mobility was only attained by extreme discipline and organization, for which the Romans were justly famous.

Even before the army's reorganization, when the legion had been larger – about 6,000 men – and considerably less flexible, it had been sufficiently mobile to defeat the Macedonian phalanx. With its increased mobility it was far too powerful a machine for the barbarian tribes of Europe to handle, however numerous they were. By the time of the Emperor Augustus, the Roman army consisted of almost 30 legions, with very nearly as many auxiliaries in reserve.

The legionaries, as the individual soldiers were called, were all equipped with a large rectangular shield (*scutum*). This was slightly convex in order to provide protection round the body. Instead of being used to overlap each other, as the Greek hoplite shields had been used, the Roman shields were held edge to edge, as the legionaries advanced, presenting an impenetrable barrier. The famous Roman short sword (*gladius*) was usually held on the right side, so as not to get in the way of the shield. Each legionary also carried a javelin (*pilum*) with a long iron point, a sharp addition to his effectiveness.

The helmet was lighter than that of the hoplites; it did not have the nose-guard, though it retained the cheek pieces. Sometimes only a breastplate was worn, with strips of leather hanging like a skirt to give lower protection; sometimes body armour of mail (*lorica*) stretched down to waist or thigh. Greaves were generally worn only by those in the front of the battle line. Those behind, requiring to be more mobile, preferred to do without them.

The Tough Test of Civil War

At the height of their power the Roman legions were put to the test not so much by the barbarian enemies of the Roman people but by internal war. Roman legions strove against each other with sophisticated tactics in which both sides were well experienced but against which neither side had come as yet in battle. The war machine confronted itself on the battlefield. It was a novel experience.

Hitherto the Gallic and Germanic tribes had put up fierce but ineffectual resistance. The advance of the Roman machine had been steady determined and inevitable, and Roman losses had been slight in comparison. It was not until

A Roman centurion looks over his legionnaires, who are armed with a rectangular shield, short sword and javelin. Helmet, breastplate and shoulder armour complete their equipment.

the civil wars that the machine began to suffer real damage.

Julius Caesar's confrontation with Pompey at Pharsalus, in Thessaly, in 48 B.C. was an important battle in the history of Rome. Despite vastly superior cavalry and an army double the size, Pompey was defeated and Caesar's authority re-established. It was a tactical victory in which Caesar used his forces most effectively by holding back his reserve cohorts until the last moment. By that time Pompey's cavalry had expended their effort against Caesar's first lines and had been thrown back in confusion by a previously prepared flanking movement. As the flanking cohorts struck Pompey's army, Caesar's main reserves attacked through his first line.

The ensuing rout resulted in surrender by the larger part of Pompey's army.

The Fortified Roman Camp

The Roman legion was able to march about 15–16 miles a day. On campaign, fortified camps were constructed at frequent intervals along the route. These acted as protection for the night, to cover the rear of an advancing army and, when fortified more strongly, as outposts of the Empire. They were fortified according to the permanence of their position. But their layout and organization were rigidly established and, since the Roman legion spent a great deal of its time in encampment, these camps became an integral part of the Roman military machine.

Remains of camps can still be seen in Europe and Britain today. Sometimes these merely take the form of earthworks but occasionally the remains of solid fortifications have been found, as at Richborough, England, in the picture.

The Human Tortoise

The legionary himself had one very useful and interesting function in any attack on an enemy fortification well-guarded by walls of any height. The human 'tortoise', or clambering device, was a machine of war as important and effective as the scaling ladder and the grappling hook. By bending down and holding their shields hori-

zontally above them, several legionaries could provide a platform on which their companions could stand in order to scale the wall.

Marching in tight formation and crouched under their shields, the legionaries were also well protected from the javelins, arrows and stones that rained down on them from above as they advanced toward the fortification.

The Lost Legions

Adaptability was the key to the legion's success, as it must be to the continued success of any machine. So when, slowly, the Germanic tribes began to learn from their successful adversaries and the Romans themselves failed to adapt to

frontier conditions while simultaneously finding those frontiers overstretched and themselves torn apart by further internal wars, the Roman machine faltered, began to break up and gradually collapsed.

This collapse took place steadily over two to three hundred years. But it began when German auxiliary soldiers, tribesmen under Roman jurisdiction, rose up under their leader Arminius against the Roman commander Varus in A.D. 9. Varus could not adapt to the guerilla-style warfare of the German tribesmen. He lost three legions to the Germans in the Teutoberger Forest: from that moment the legion ceased to be an invincible machine.

A THOUSAND YEARS OF SIEGE DEVICES
The Forts Become Stronger

The legion was not the only Roman contribution to the art of war; the Romans also developed siege artillery of powerful and varied ability. Before the invention of gunpowder, the motive forces available to propel large missiles into an enemy stronghold, or to gain access to that stronghold, gave rise to an odd-looking assortment of machines. As we have already seen, the Assyrians used covered battering rams and assault towers almost 2,000 years before Christ. The Macedonians used catapult artillery 300–400 years before Christ. And similar machines were still being used, alongside some of the earliest cannon, when the Turks besieged Constantinople in A.D. 1453.

Siege machines developed side-by-side with the development of fortifications. Earthworks gave way to constructions of stone, with thicker and thicker walls, deeper and wider ditches and an increasing number of towers and turrets, in order to combat machines aimed at scaling the walls, crossing the ditches and bombarding within the fortress.

There were three main types of machine that evolved for propelling missiles. Each used a different source of power. The catapult of the Macedonians used torque provided by twisted ropes. The trebuchet, used by the Romans and late into the Middle Ages, worked on counterbalancing weights. And the spring engine employed the flexibility of wood.

Catapult and Spring-engine

The Romans developed a comprehensive siege train in which the catapult played a major part. This was the conventional catapult that used a single arm on which the missile was placed. The arm was held between thick, twisted ropes. Torque, or twisted tension, increased as the arm was pulled down. This was virtually the same as the Macedonian torsion catapult, although the Romans often called it an *onager*, which was another word for wild ass.

There was another form of Roman catapult that was lighter than the onager and used more often in the field against enemy soldiers than against fortifications. This catapult had two smaller arms, each slotted into twisted ox-sinew and fitted on either side of the shaft up which the missile ran. Rope, or sinew, joined the outstretched ends of the arms like a bow; the missile was fitted into the arc of the sinew. Power was

derived from the torque of the twisted sinews and from the flexibility of the arms when the missile was drawn back in preparation for firing. In this machine the missile was likely to be an arrow, javelin or large spear. The machine could be adjusted to provide a certain angle of accuracy.

A third variation dispensed with the twisted rope in favour of a large metal bow. This type of 'ballista' grew in complexity during the Middle Ages until sometimes two or three bows were used on the same machine. The principle of the device was like a giant crossbow and the power was derived from the tension in the metal. Like the onager, the ballista could hurl large stones with great force a distance of 300–400 yards.

The spring-engine also used the tension of wood or metal and was primarily used to fire arrows. The arrow rested on one piece of wood, with the flight end of the arrow projecting slightly behind the wood. Another piece of flexible wood, lying upright against the first piece, was bound tightly to the first piece at its base. The top of the second piece of wood was then drawn back under great tension by a rope and winch. It was then released sharply so that it sprang back against the base of the arrow, which shot from its resting place with armour-penetrating force.

It may not seem that this would be a very accurate device but some degree of accuracy was attained either by resting the arrow in a groove or, more often, by shooting it through a hole in the support. Various ingenious ways of altering its angle of inclination included a hinged rest for the arrow that could be raised or lowered on a series of stepped sockets.

One of the most telling modifications of the spring-engine was a multiple battery of arrows fired simultaneously. The system was the same as on the single shot machine, using holes in the support for the arrows. A large piece of wood was drawn back and struck against a board on which were set several rows of arrows. The consequent rain of arrows on the enemy could, as might be imagined, tear a gap in their ranks with fearful and dispiriting effect.

The Powerful Trebuchet

The *trebuchet* was used in wars all over Europe and Asia Minor for over 1,500 years. One of the most powerful of the ancient siege machines, it could hurl stones weighing anything up to two to three hundredweight over several hundred

Above: The lighter form of Roman catapult, using two arms fixed in twisted sinews.

A spring-engine, complete with steps for elevation.

yards and over the highest walls and ditches.

The principle of the trebuchet was very simple. A long arm was set on a pivot so that it had a longer and a shorter end. The pivot was supported by a solid frame. At its shorter end the arm was weighted by a large box full of earth or stones. The box was hinged to the end of the arm so that, as the arm moved up and down, the contents of the box would not fall out. The longer end of the arm held the missile – usually in a sling – and was drawn down against the weight of the box at the other end by a winch or capstan. When the long end was released, the weight at the short end swung the long end up and the missile was flung through the air.

Missiles varied from rocks and barrels of burning tar to the putrescent corpses of friend and foe. These not only demoralized the opposition but were likely to spread disease. Such drastic action was generally a last resort, even before the days of supposed chivalry, but nonetheless was a recognized and effective method of shortening a siege.

Both besieged and besiegers used trebuchets. The missiles of the besieged could create considerable disruption in the camp of the enemy, on grouped soldiers, on mobile wickerwork shields, on assault towers and on covered battering rams, as well as on the opposing missile machines. Just as important, the trebuchet could be used to disrupt the construction of these devices, which were generally put together on the spot out of available materials.

A medieval trebuchet being winched down, ready for loading. Rocks used for missiles are lying on the ground.

A Besieger's Basket

There were other, less common devices used in siegecraft, such as a specially designed besieger's basket and a boring machine for tunnelling. The basket was made of wickerwork, sometimes covered by animal hides. It was held over the soldier and completely covered his body. There was an eyeslit to the front. The basket served much the same purpose as the Roman tortoise, to guard the soldier against arrows and stones as he approached the fortification; unlike the tortoise, this was an individual defence.

The boring machine was at first a wooden screw (later and more effectively made of metal) for penetrating beneath the foundations of a wall. A machine of this kind is mentioned in various Roman records but it seems uncertain as to what its motive power was other than sheer human effort. It is possible that at a later stage a system of cogs could have enabled a horse to provide the necessary power.

The Siege of Constantinople

Major siege machines such as the trebuchet continued in use throughout the Middle Ages. The Mongols made use of trebuchets in their amazing surge through Asia at the end of the 12th Century A.D.; so did the Byzantine armies of the 7th Century and so did the European combatants during the 100 Years War of the 14th Century. The Crusaders used them at the successful siege of Jerusalem in 1099 and one of their last effective appearances was side by side with the first great cannon at the siege of Constantinople by the Turkish Sultan, Mahomet, in 1453.

Over 700 years earlier, in A.D. 717, an attempt by the Moslems to take Constantinople had failed, partly because they underestimated the extent of siegecraft necessary to capture such a well-fortified and heavily defended citadel. Mahomet did not make the same mistake. His siege lasted several weeks and it sealed the fate of the Byzantine Empire.

It had been Mahomet's ambition, even before he became Sultan, to capture Constantinople, which by the middle of the 15th Century was only hanging by its teeth to the last vestiges of Byzantine power in the eastern Mediterranean. The Turks had already thrust north as close as Adrianople by the time Mahomet's father died in 1451. At once Mahomet determined to realize his ambition and to overthrow the unbelievers, whose ruler, Constantine XI, saw the danger but was unable to gather any real support for his

Above: Mahomet II, who conquered Constantinople in A.D. 1453.
Right: Roman soldiers forming a tortoise with their shields as they approach the walls of a besieged fortress.

threatened city from his sadly bashful allies.

Constantine had fewer than 10,000 soldiers with which to defend the city and not all of these could be relied on. His only hope lay in the strength of his fortifications and the skill and experience of his Genoese commander Giustiniani. On the landward side, the city was protected by a ditch and a triple wall with nine gates. On the seaward side, natural defences combined with artificial ones to present an inaccessible face. A huge chain stretched across the mouth of the Golden Horn, which itself provided a defence from that side.

Against this solid guard, Mahomet had an army well over ten times as large, led by his

superbly trained Janissaries. He had a fleet of
about 300 ships with which to blockade the city
from the sea and, most important of all, he had a
vast siege-train of catapults, trebuchets, assault
towers and a number of monster brass cannon.
The siege of Constantinople was to be the first
major artillery bombardment in history. Ancient
and modern machines opened fire together at the
beginning of April, 1453.

On April 18, Mahomet launched his first
assault on the landward side of the city, but his
artillery had not then prepared a sufficient
breach in the walls. Giustiniani repelled the
Turks with a concentrated fire of small arms and
a barrage of missiles from his own catapults and

from the guns ranged along the battlements.

A further setback to the Turks occurred when
four Genoese vessels appeared in the Bosporus
and succeeded in beating aside the massed
Turkish fleet that was blockading the entrance to
the Golden Horn. After several hours of fierce
combat, the four ships gained the safety of the
Horn itself.

Enraged at being snubbed a second time,
Mahomet determined on the astounding project
of seizing the Golden Horn by dragging 70–80 of
his own ships 10 miles overland from the Bosporus. A timber track was laid, greased with the
fat of sheep and oxen, and the vessels were
hauled by bullocks and slaves.

The 'City-taker'

With the city by then totally surrounded, Mahomet renewed his attacks. Every breach he made in the walls was quickly repaired by the defenders; every assault on the gates along the landward side was fiercely rebuffed. In one determined onslaught the Turks dragged forward a vast mobile wooden tower, complete with a whole series of platforms, ladders, protective shields, artillery and soldiers. This was the great 'helepolis', or 'city-taker'.

The helepolis was so huge that it overlooked one of the breaches in the wall. The Turks within the tower were able to pour a damaging rain of stones, arrows and gunfire on the defenders as they desperately tried to repair the breach. This engagement lasted all day, until the gallant defenders rolled a number of gunpowder barrels into the ditch beneath the helepolis and blew it and all it contained into little pieces.

Attempts at undermining the walls also failed. The Byzantines counter-mined and the mines of the Turks collapsed; or else the Turks were drowned when their mines were flooded, or they were suffocated by stink bombs, or beaten back by hand to hand fighting in the cramped passages.

Every check caused Mahomet greater anger and greater concern. His supplies had not anticipated a long siege; by the middle of May they were running short. On May 29 he launched his final desperate attack, with 10,000 Janissaries and nearly a quarter of a million tribesmen – against about 4,000 surviving Byzantines.

The first attackers died in the ditches and against the walls. The next wave used their bodies as platforms. A breach in one part of the wall enabled a group of Janissaries to launch a flanking attack on the weakening defenders. At the moment of crisis, Giustiniani was badly wounded. Then Constantine himself fell as he led a final attempt to halt the Turks.

That was the end of the defence. The Turks entered the city and indulged in an orgy of killing, looting and destruction. Mahomet had won his coveted prize and the Western world stood shocked by the loss.

An artist's impression of the Siege of Constantinople, picturing Christianity overwhelmed by the massive forces of the infidel.

ELEPHANTS IN BATTLE
Chinese War Elephants

It was in China, so far as we know, that elephants were used for the first time in war. In their size, the thickness of their hides and the terror they were able to instil in an enemy, they were surely one of the forerunners of the modern tank.

The Shang dynasty, who established their civilization along the Yellow River, where men had already been living for 20,000 years, dominated North China for about 600 years. They were finally driven out by the Chou, in the 12th Century B.C. Whether or not the elephants were the secret weapon that proved to be the decisive turning point in the series of battles that brought about the downfall of the Shang dynasty, we do not know, but we do know that elephants were used during these encounters.

We can imagine the effect that the elephants had from the more detailed accounts of their reappearance and use in Asia Minor 800 years later. The armies of Alexander the Great returned with elephants from their campaigns in India. On Alexander's death, elephants were used by the armies that fought over the division of his empire and contributed to its break-up.

Elephants Across the Alps

Over a hundred years later war elephants made what was probably their most celebrated appearance – in Hannibal's campaigns against the Romans. This was the Second Punic War between Carthage and Rome, which lasted from 218–202 B.C. Dominating the western end of the Mediterranean, Carthage posed a threat to the power of Rome, that Rome could not ignore. Anticipating a Roman attack, Hannibal took the offensive.

In October 218 BC, Hannibal crossed the Alps with 30,000 men and 60 elephants to catch the Romans by surprise and lay waste the plains of Northern Italy, while the main Roman forces were on their way to Spain to attack the Carthaginian base. Hannibal showed immense courage and skill in taking the battle into enemy land and succeeded in getting his army through the narrow, snow-covered passes against the opposition of local tribesmen accustomed to the terrain. The elephants proved the greatest problem of all. Totally unused to such conditions and terrified by the narrowness of the tracks and the dizzy heights, many panicked and caused accidents.

Once across, Hannibal's tactic was vindicated and, with the help of his elephants, he defeated several large Roman armies. His greatest victory

Above: Hannibal's army ferried itself and its elephants across the Rhône in a daring manoeuvre to surprise the Romans. Makeshift rafts of wood were used, supported by blown-up pig-skins, a technique that the Assyrians had also used, centuries before.

Below: An impression of the route of Hannibal's courageous and successful march through the Alps, which enabled him to gain dramatic victories in Northern Italy. The route goes from Vizelle (left) to Turin (right). Hannibal's camps are marked with short, thick lines along the route.

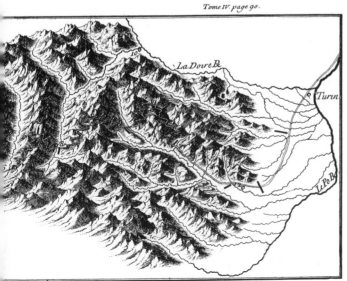

Tome IV. page 90.

was at the Battle of Cannae, in 216 B.C. The Roman force of 65,000 was virtually wiped out.

Perhaps the part played by the elephants in these victories should not be over-emphasized. They did undoubtedly present a formidable sight and they were certainly well armoured. They wore a large overall covering of leather, with an additional piece on the forehead and leather or cloth to protect the vulnerable area below the ears. Around their chests they wore heavy chain metal protection and there were rings of metal round their legs and sometimes round parts of their trunk. The turrets on their backs usually contained archers and spearmen; the elephant itself could, of course, inflict considerable damage with its tusks, with the sheer weight of its bulk and the trampling of its feet.

But the prime purpose of these giant war machines was to instil panic in the opposition. And to the common legionary, however well-disciplined, these monsters were at first sight a very dreadful apparition. It proved, however, that the dreadful apparition could turn with terrible effect on the very people for whom it was meant to be fighting. War elephants were not easy to handle. They were intelligent creatures but were not inclined to attack unless enraged. So it was necessary first to excite them and, once excited, they were as likely to trample friend as foe.

The Battle of Zama

Scipio the Younger used this weakness when he finally crushed the Carthaginian army at the Battle of Zama in 202 B.C. Once the Roman troops had become accustomed to the elephants they were able to scare them in turn and send them bolting back into their own ranks. One story relates that Scipio terrified Hannibal's elephants by sending a herd of pigs among them. Those elephants that did reach the leading Roman cohorts were left to pass through the gaps between the legions, whence they trundled harmlessly away. Outflanking the Carthaginians with his cavalry, Scipio assured himself of victory.

Confidence in the war elephant declined after this defeat, for the use of them depended essentially on surprise and fear for success. When they lost these advantages, they became too cumbersome and too unreliable. After the 1st Century A.D., they were no longer used in the Mediterranean area or in Europe, although they have been used in India until recent centuries.

THE MOUNTED KNIGHT
Saddle and Stirrup

The heavily armoured mounted knight threatened to dominate the medieval battlefields of Europe. He was a moving fortress that sprouted offensive weapons – lance, sword and mace – with which to smash down the forces of opposition. In a dense charge, the ordinary foot-soldier could not withstand him; as a roving, individual combatant, he could do what he liked. He was a fully-armed, fully-armoured, fully-mobile fighting machine.

Mounted horsemen had been used in preference to chariots 1,000 years before Christ. A mounted soldier could manoeuvre far more easily than one on foot. The Assyrians used mounted archers and spearmen; so did the Phrygians and Scythians of Asia Minor, in about 500 B.C. The Macedonians and the Romans both used cavalry. But in all cases the horsemen were lightly protected and used neither saddle nor stirrup.

Without these essential pieces of equipment, the early cavalryman was easily dismounted, and could not deliver a blow with the full force of his body behind it. Both saddle and stirrup seem to have originated in China but it is difficult to conclude when precisely they came to Europe and Asia Minor. It is generally accepted that some of the tribes in Gaul possessed saddles of a kind in about A.D. 100–200. Stirrups appeared later. They were certainly in use in the 8th Century but they may have come into use in a simpler form in the Byzantine Empire even earlier. There is evidence of their use at the end of the 6th Century in the 'Art of War' of the Byzantine Emperor Maurice Tiberius.

The Byzantine Cataphracts

It was the Byzantine army, committed to a vigorous and aggressive foreign policy under the Emperor Justinian and led by the brilliant commander Belisarius during the middle of the 6th Century, that first made good use of fully armoured cavalry. Belisarius's élite horsemen, the Cataphracts, were well-equipped, well-trained and superior to almost any troops they encountered.

The Cataphracts were clothed entirely in scale armour or mail, which was also used to protect their horses. They were armed usually with a bow, a sword and a spear. Similar cavalry used by the Persians sometimes had the added protection of a beautifully worked visor that covered

Above: A horseman from the decorated palace of Guzana, with helmet and shield but no stirrups.
Right: Cataphract with carefully moulded face mask and a complete covering of scale armour for himself and his horse.

the whole face and followed its contours to form a remarkable face mask.

Scale armour consisted of many rows of overlapping scales secured on the undersurface to a tough lining. Until plate armour came into general use in the 14th Century, scale armour was the only alternative to chain mail, although during the 11th and 12th Centuries mail and scale armour were often combined to give additional protection. The advantage of mail was its flexibility, although it was a tedious job to produce since every ring had to be woven individually into the coat. Each ring interlocked with four surrounding rings and was secured by having its ends flattened, drilled and rivetted together. One of the disadvantages of mail was that a powerful blow by an adversary could sever the links and drive the sharp-ended pieces of metal wire into the body of the wearer. His own armour therefore, at times, became more dangerous to him than the sword of his enemy. In order to protect himself, the knight often wore a well-padded garment beneath his mail.

The Knights of Charles Martel

Under the Carolingians of the 8th Century A.D. the knight became not only an important part of the army but an integral part of the feudal structure of society as well, as the definition of 'feudal' suggests: 'the holding of land for military service'. Charles Martel increased his power in France by distributing land (seized from the Church) to his vassals, in return for which they guaranteed to turn up – fully equipped – on demand, together with an agreed number of followers, ready to join any proposed campaign. It was with an army shaped of this material that Charles Martel managed to stem the advance of the Arabs through Europe at the Battle of Poitiers, in AD 732 – and so avert a major disaster.

Poitiers was an important turning point in European history. The Arab threat was diminished and Carolingian power established. Charles Martel's heavy cavalry, equipped with stirrups and high saddles played a large part in the victory and the subsequent expansion of the Empire that Charlemagne took to even greater heights and established with authority.

With the aid of his stirrups, the knight could virtually stand up, leaning his whole weight forward, and thrusting with his legs. By this means the full force of his horse's impetus could be brought behind the knight's lance, which became a personal battering ram, lethally tipped, and capable of great penetration. Meanwhile, the high saddle, with pommel to the front and cantle behind, kept the knight firmly on his horse, despite the shock of his own charge and the blows of his adversaries. There was a danger that the lance would stick in the target, either breaking or twisting the knight from his saddle. This was averted by a small cross-bar or pennant just behind the point of the lance, that stopped the lance from penetrating too deeply.

Helmets and Plate Armour

Norman knights of the 11th Century and Italian knights of the 12th Century all wore scale armour, sometimes as coats that stretched down to their knees. Loose-fitting surcoats often covered the armour and served the double purpose of a distinguishing mark and an additional protection against sword cuts; the folds of the material greatly reduced the direct force of the blow.

From the simple conical helmet with a *nasal* (a protection for the nose), there developed more elaborate face-plates that eventually formed a helmet that covered the face totally, as well as

protecting both the front and the back of the neck. It was provided with eyeslits and ventilation holes. It is difficult to imagine that either of these were very efficient. Range of vision was greatly limited, rather as if blinkers were being worn not only to the sides but above and below the eyes as well. Anyone who has ever taken fencing lessons and knows how hot a mesh fencing mask can become after only a few moments exercise may be able to imagine what it must have been like inside a solid metal cannister after several *hours* of battle!

Another protective device was a breastplate or waistcoat of *cuir bouilli*, which was made of leather boiled and pressed and made additionally stiff with wax. But the classic 'knight in armour' wore plate mail, which began to become popular at the end of the 13th Century and developed into increasingly heavy and complex styles over the next three centuries.

Plate armour began with plates of metal inserted into a leather or cloth garment. Plate covers for knees (*poleyn*), shins (*chausse*) and elbows (*couter*) followed. By the end of the 13th Century, gauntlets were made of plate metal and gorgets, to protect the neck, were in general use.

During this century horses were also covered in curtains of mail. With both rider and horse virtually unrecognizable within their armour,

Left: This stone-carving of Roland represents one of the most famous of all the Carolingian knights, whose death in the pass of Roncevalles in 778 began a legend. Charlemagne's army was defeated by an ambush, but his knights subsequently helped him to establish a powerful empire.
Right: This richly ornamented helmet is from the Anglo-Saxon ship burial at Sutton Hoo in Britain's East Anglia. The date of the burial – a king's treasure in a Viking longboat—has been estimated between 650 and 670. Other weapons found at the site included a sword with a gold and garnet pommel, a shield, a mail coat, an iron-handled axe, some javelins, spears and a knife.

ODO EPS:BACVLV TEN

An incident from the Bayeux Tapestry, showing Norman knights advancing into Battle. The Tapestry was created to commemorate the Norman invasion of Britain in 1066.

there was an increased necessity to wear some kind of distinguishing marks. 'Heraldry' goes back to the Greeks and Romans, and even earlier. The elaborate system of medieval heraldry began properly in the 12th Century and spread widely in the 13th Century. Family marks appeared on shields, surcoats and helmets and added a touch of gaiety to the austere clank of metal.

Gradually plate armour covered the entire body, elaborately hinged and designed to make the blows of the enemy glance off. The names of the various pieces of armour conjure up a romantic picture far removed from the agonies of the battlefield. *Solerets* were broad, plated shoes; the *cuisse* were the thigh guards; *tassets*, a kind of plated skirt, overlapped the cuisse; and *taces*, bands of plate linked to allow flexibility, protected waist and stomach. Underneath the tassets and behind the joints of the limbs, there was often an additional protection of chain mail. A *vambrace* protected the forearm and a *rerebrace* the upper arm; the shoulders were guarded by heavy *pauldrons* with a *haute-piece* projecting up to give extra protection to the neck. The helmet usually had a visor that could be raised either by hinges at the side of the head or by a single hinge at the top.

There was never any one style of armour that was at any time universally worn. Styles came and went according to need as much as fashion and different countries had very different designs. For instance, the more rounded shape of 15th-Century Italian design, with a lance rest fixed to the right side of the breastplate, was a good deal plainer than German design of the later part of that century. In German Gothic armour there were many flutings, which gave the armour extra strength and helped to deflect the assailant's weapon. A later German style was known as 'Maximilian' and was characterized by a series of ridges over the entire armour, with the exception of the greaves.

The Obsolete Knight

During the 16th Century heavy cavalry still wore armour; indeed some of the heaviest armour, weighing up to 90 pounds, was worn at this time. But firearms had already rendered the armoured knight an outdated machine. Driven to protecting himself more and more fully from the threat of crossbow and longbow, he could not resist the force of shot backed by gunpowder, however much armour he adopted. And although armour was still used in the English Civil War of the

Above: Armoured knights clash at the Battle of Auray, between John de Montford (left) and Charles de Blois (on the ground). The battle was in 1364, during the Anglo-French 100 Years War Right: The 15th-Century Italian knight has a rest for his lance attached to his breast-plate, and is carrying a mace.

mid-17th Century and the European 30 Years War of the first half of that century it became much lighter; by the middle of the next century, protection was reduced to half-armour.

For a time the charge of the armoured knight had been an irresistible force. Foot-soldiers could only hope to cut the horse from under him; they had no hope of standing up against him. He could roam where he liked, killing where he felt inclined. The clash of two bodies of knights was probably the most awe-inspiring sight the battlefields of Europe had ever seen. In every way the armoured knight dominated his surroundings. The disappearance of this formidable machine, through the force of progress, brought to an end a style of warfare and an attitude of life.

THE DEADLY QUARREL OF THE CROSSBOW
The Little Ballista

The knight was countered at first by the crossbow, which probably originated in the East and was known, in a modified form, to the Romans. Its other name, 'arbalest', comes from the Latin 'arcu', a bow, and 'ballista', an engine of war. The Romans made good use of the full-size ballista but do not seem to have exploited the full potential of its smaller relation.

This potential was not realized until the 11th and 12th Centuries, when armoured knights became increasingly dominant in European warfare. The crossbow enabled an unarmoured man to knock down a mounted knight from a safe distance. The realization that the knight was no longer invulnerable – worse still, that the inferior infantryman now possessed a machine that could penetrate the knight's armour – shocked the Orders of Chivalry. What frightened them even more was the realization that they themselves could not use the machine in retaliation from horseback. Their disadvantage was irremediable and their demise assured.

The Crossbow is Banned

In a last ditch attempt to stem the spread of this insidious threat, the Pope spoke out against the crossbow. In 1139, the Second Lateran Council banned the use of the new machine in civilized warfare; they called it an atrocity. There was, however, a proviso – a proviso that was to be echoed when the first machine gun was introduced: although it was forbidden to use the crossbow against fellow Christians, it could freely be used against the infidel Moslem.

The Crusaders used the crossbow to good enough effect against the Saracens, particularly during the Third Crusade. Richard Cœur de Lion's victory at Arsuf, in 1191, was greatly assisted by the chaos caused amongst the enemy by his crossbowmen. But the papal interdict against the crossbow did not restrict it to the Middle East for long; it was far too useful a machine. By the late 13th Century the crossbowmen of France and Spain were an important branch of the army and were recognized as such. Genoese crossbowmen, often hired as mercenaries, made their mark on the battlefields of the early 14th Century, until tested against the English longbow at the Battle of Crécy, in 1346.

One great advantage of the crossbow was that its use did not require much training on the part of the bowman, nor did it require the

The crossbow was powerful but tedious to load

strength necessary to the longbowman. The early wooden crossbow was drawn back by hand but the later and more effective steel bow required a winch to 'span' or draw it. The bow consisted of a short cross-arm mounted on a stock, with a groove cut along the stock to guide the missile and a trigger by which to release it. While the bowman used both hands on the winch, he held the bow steady by placing his foot in the stirrup at the front.

Rewinding the bow was a slow and vulnerable job. The bowman had to stand upright and was therefore fully exposed to enemy fire during the operation. In consequence, Genoese bowmen were well protected with body armour and sometimes had a companion to hold a large shield before them while they reloaded.

The slow rate of fire was perhaps the crossbow's greatest disadvantage. It could fire little more than one shot a minute. Also, it was not

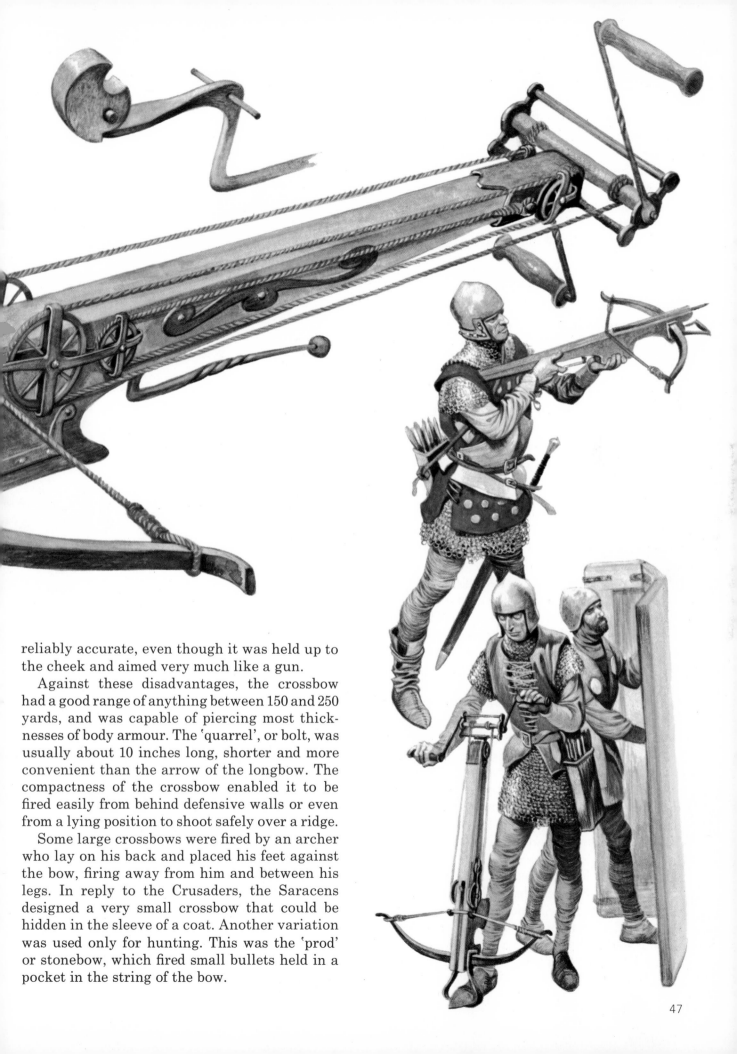

reliably accurate, even though it was held up to the cheek and aimed very much like a gun.

Against these disadvantages, the crossbow had a good range of anything between 150 and 250 yards, and was capable of piercing most thicknesses of body armour. The 'quarrel', or bolt, was usually about 10 inches long, shorter and more convenient than the arrow of the longbow. The compactness of the crossbow enabled it to be fired easily from behind defensive walls or even from a lying position to shoot safely over a ridge.

Some large crossbows were fired by an archer who lay on his back and placed his feet against the bow, firing away from him and between his legs. In reply to the Crusaders, the Saracens designed a very small crossbow that could be hidden in the sleeve of a coat. Another variation was used only for hunting. This was the 'prod' or stonebow, which fired small bullets held in a pocket in the string of the bow.

47

THE CLOTHYARD SHAFT OF THE LONGBOW
From Cavemen to Hastings

The crossbow and the longbow fought out many conflicts during the 13th and 14th Centuries. The longbow had a far greater rate of fire and, in the hands of an expert, greater range and accuracy as well.

Bows of one shape or another had, of course, been used for thousands of years, first by the Egyptians, Assyrians and in China, then by the Persians, Greeks and Macedonians, later by the Moslems and even the Vikings. It is perhaps surprising that the Romans never made more use of the bow. There are arrowheads surviving from Paleolithic and Neolithic times. And, in more recent American history, the American Indians made highly effective use of bows and arrows against the early settlers.

Self bows were made of one material only – a stave of wood, for example. If more than one piece of the same material was used in the bow, it was called a built bow. A composite bow consisted of several different materials glued together, such as wood, horn and animal sinew. These were the common variations of bow in early times. The first English bows were quite short, but the Normans arrived in 1066 with a medium length bow, which in combination with their cavalry gave them victory at the Battle of Hastings and the conquest of Britain.

At first King Harold of the Saxons held back the Norman infantry attacks against the hill-top on which he set up his defence. His formidable wall of shields and the threatening sweep of his long axes proved impenetrable, until Duke William broke the line by luring the Saxons down the slope and into the open by a feigned retreat. Caught beneath a rain of high-angled arrows, the Saxons were cut apart by the Norman cavalry charge, as the famous Bayeux Tapestry so vividly shows. It is clear from that picture what an important part the bowmen played in the battle. And it was an arrow – so for a long time the story was told, though now it is questioned – that decided the outcome by piercing King Harold fatally in the eye.

The Welsh Longbow

The so-called 'English' longbow should be called the Welsh longbow, since the true origin of the bow that dominated the 100 Years' War in Europe, and has become an integral part of the emotional saga of English history, was Wales. In 1120, Welsh archers ambushed the English under

Above: A statuette of an early Etruscan warrior drawing his bow, possibly from Sardinia.

Right: The English longbowmen on the right face the Genoese crossbowmen on the left at the decisive Battle of Crécy in 1346. The crossbowman was virtually defenceless during the slow process of reloading. It was the longbow that won the day.

Henry II, near Powys. A hundred years later the longbow was in common use in England. By 1250, Edward I had wisely ensured that the longbow was part of the standard equipment of his army.

Unlike the crossbow, the longbow took years of practice and great strength to use effectively. The bow was about six feet long, as tall as a man or taller, with a linen or hemp bowstring. The clothyard shaft, or arrow, was about three feet long, fledged, or feathered, with goose feathers and pointed with a small, sharp head that would deliver the greatest possible impact on the smallest possible area. Peacock feathers were sometimes used for special peacetime occasions.

The longbow could fire about six times faster than the crossbow – that is, about six aimed shots a minute – with an effective range of 200 yards, although an experienced archer may have been

able to fire almost twice that distance. The bow had a pull of about 100 pounds and, to string it, the bowman usually bent the bow between his legs. To fire the bow, the string was drawn back to the ear; because of the great pull, the knack was to put the weight of the body *into* the bow with the left arm.

The bow itself was made of yew and the growth of these trees was encouraged, although hickory, ash and elm were also used. The manufacture and sale of bows was carefully controlled from about the middle of the 13th Century and, from the age of 15, all able-bodied Englishmen were compelled to train with the bow regularly. Archery practice was at one time made compulsory on Sundays.

Victory over the Crossbow

The relative merits of longbow and crossbow were tested at Crécy, where the English proved that a force of infantry and archers in an extended position could stand against an advancing force of mounted knights. Preceded by a ragged line of Genoese crossbowmen, the French cavalry approached the waiting English line. Strictly disciplined, the English held their fire until the enemy were well within range. Their rain of arrows sent the Genoese tottering back to be cut down by their own lines. The cavalry had no better effect on the solid English line of archers and footsoldiers. At the end of the day nearly 10,000 French were lost; on the English side barely 200 went down.

The French did not learn their lesson. At Poitiers, in 1356, and at Agincourt, in 1415, the English longbowman twice proved his worth against the armoured knight.

49

SWISS PIKES AND MERCENARIES
Keeping the Knights at a Distance

The knight became the butt of every new device and tactic on the battlefield simply because of the threat he himself posed. The Swiss infantry, brought together in an uneasy alliance between the various cantons against the threat of external forces, were the first soldiers in Europe to introduce the use of long-shafted weapons against mounted knights. While the armies of other countries adopted, instead of the crossbow and longbow, the pistol and handgun, the Swiss continued to achieve such astonishing successes with their long pikes that they became in great demand as mercenaries on all sides of the religious wars that savaged Europe for almost 200 years.

The Swiss pike was 18–21 feet long, with a sturdy shaft of ash and a long steel head. Its full effect was not achieved as an individual weapon but in a massed formation. Forced against their will during the second half of the 15th Century to confront the invading armies of France and Austria in decisive battles on the plains, the Swiss pikemen adopted a phalanx formation similar to the Greek pattern. As a military machine, the formation proved equally effective.

The ranks of the formation were staggered so that an impenetrable barrier of points was presented against a cavalry charge; the extreme length of the pikes enabled the pikemen to keep the horsemen beyond the effective range of their pistols. The length of a pike may seem to be an absurdly short range at which to miss with a pistol but early guns were not reliable and considerable skill was required to fire with any degree of accuracy from astride a galloping horse anxious to avoid becoming embedded on a steel bank of points.

Like a Roman legion, the Swiss phalanx was highly disciplined and could manoeuvre rapidly. Drill had to be precise in order to manipulate with any success a company of men 30–40 across and almost 100 deep. When standing against an enemy charge, they held the end of their pike against their foot and leant into the length of the pike in order to withstand the shock of impact without being pushed over.

After resounding successes against the French, first at Morat, in 1476, and a year later at Nancy, where the French King Charles the Bold was himself killed, other armies adapted the pike to their own use. In slightly modified forms it remained an integral part of many armies until the

17th Century and proved a useful weapon.

Maurice of Orange equipped the Dutch army with pikemen in about 1600, when he was trying to push the Spanish out of his country. After careful study of the Roman legions, Maurice interspersed his pikemen with musketeers, so that the former acted primarily as cover for the latter, particularly as the musketeers reloaded.

In the English Civil War of the 1640s, pikemen were used in a similar capacity to protect valuable musketeers, and during the 30 Years War that came to an end in Europe in 1648, the French used pikemen extensively.

The Gaudy Landsknechts
Meanwhile the Swiss had been hiring them-

Ucello was renowned for the decorative quality of his paintings which found an appropriate subject in the gaudy trappings depicted in The Battle of San Romano, *painted about 1456.*

selves out to whomever could pay them well enough. In the paintings of the period, dense with the rich pattern of infantry and cavalry marching seemingly in every direction or struggling in combat, there are always to be seen, like tall ears of wheat or barley, the multiple fences of the pikes rising above the heads of the contestants or lowering rank upon rank to receive and repel a new assault.

Among the most outrageous and colourful of those who wielded the pike for one nation or another during these years were the so-called *Landsknechts*. These were the real mercenaries, usually German, sometimes Swiss – the Emperor Maximilian I of Austria recruited a body of German Landsknechts agains the Swiss them-

selves in about 1500 – who enjoyed their independence and flaunted gaudy trappings to their armour. Besides pike and short fighting sword they wielded, with terrible effect, a great two-handed sword that often stood over five and a half feet high.

Swiss discipline and ferocity – for which they were equally famous – made a tremendous impact on the battlefields of Europe until the advent of more refined artillery pronounced their doom. In close ranks, relying on close combat, they were completely vulnerable to accurate and powerful fire from greater range. Like the English bowmen, brilliant in their time, they were a machine that had to give way to the more efficient devices of progress.

THE MEDIEVAL CASTLE
Roman Origins

The knight and his castle go together in popular imagination, but they are not inseparable. As war machines they performed very different functions.

The Romans had been the great exponents of fortifications, though the Assyrians, a thousand years earlier, had built sturdy city forts with walls sometimes 75 feet thick. Ancient Babylon was supposed to have had walls 85 feet thick. But the Romans built fortifications whose remains still stand in North Africa and whose concept and design were barely equalled in one and a half thousand years.

As with the Assyrians, it was largely the efficiency of their own siege trains that provoked the Romans into developing forts strong enough to withstand their own sophisticated methods of attack. This necessity for castles and forts to keep one step ahead of contemporary siege machines was one of the causes for the steady evolution of their design. The process of action and reaction runs through the development of almost all war machines.

Forts were essential to the Romans because of the extent of their conquests, as a result of which they found themselves trying to hold down alien and often aggressive peoples with minimal troops. The forts acted as outposts of the Empire. This continued to be their function in later centuries and for other nations: the fort acted either as an outpost or a last method of defence.

The Byzantines under Belisarius built walled towns as well as isolated forts throughout North Africa during the 6th Century A.D. One good example of a fort constructed in a commanding position is Aïn Tounga, which guards a pass in Tunisia and once controlled the area.

The motte and bailey castle was common in France during the 11th Century. The motte was a high mound in the centre of the walled area and the bailey was the area of ground between the outer walls. There would often be several lines of walls surrounding the central fort; this resulted in Inner and Outer Baileys.

Norman castles of the 11th Century still stand. Most of these were built of stone. In England, the outer shell of the Windsor Tower dates from 1075 and the rectangular White Tower, at the Tower of London dates from 1080.

Below: Windsor Castle and the Round Tower (right). Right: The Tower of London, centre of much of England's history.

The Castles of the Crusaders

The greatest boost to European castle design came from the Holy Land. The First Crusade marched against the Saracens in the last decade of the 11th Century and found them firmly entrenched and well-defended in captured Byzantine castles. Having battered their heads against Antioch and Nicaea and captured Jerusalem in 1099, the Crusaders quickly learnt their lesson and started to build their own castles in order to hold what ground they had gained in a strange and distant land where they were surrounded by the constant fear of attack by the infidel.

The Crusades lasted for over 300 years and the castles that the Crusaders built were con-

structed to last for ever. Over that period, although Crusading armies came and went, many generations were born and died in the Holy Land and knew no other home. The finest of the Crusader castles is undoubtedly Krak des Chevaliers, although there are plenty of others – at Saone, Margat and elsewhere.

The influence of the Byzantine-style castle, with its circular towers to give a better all-round view of the attacker and its retention of the *keep* or *donjon* as a last line of defence, returned to Europe with the Third Crusade. Richard I built Château Gaillard along these lines on a natural eminence 300 feet above the River Seine.

This extra height gave the castle added protection against siege machines, an important precaution after the lessons of the Holy Land. The main defences were constructed against the approach, with three baileys as three separate lines of defence. Château Gaillard fell to Philip II of France not long after it was built, but it stretched the French king to a long and expensive siege that weakened his army.

In the Holy Land the Byzantine traditions continued until the middle of the 15th Century. One of the most impressive fortifications still standing was built by the Saracens at Rumeli Hisari, commanding the northern shore of the Bosporus.

Left: Château Gaillard, built by Richard I on the lines of the Byzantine castles. It holds a commanding position on the cliff-top.
Top: The 15th-Century German Tower in the Castle of St Peter at Bodrum, in Turkey.
Above: The tower and walls of Rumeli Hisari, built by Mahomet II, the conqueror of Constantinople.

This was constructed in 1452. It has walls 24 feet thick and is said to have been built by 10,000 men in four and a half months. A year later Mahomet achieved his great ambition to capture nearby Constantinople and add it to his empire.

Castles and Cannon

Meanwhile, in England, some of the most remarkably durable castles since Roman times had been constructed under Edward I to stand guard along the border between England and Wales and to assist his conquest of the vigorously insurgent Welsh. In most cases, the central castle, square or round, was surrounded by two or more lines of walls with well-fortified circular towers at the corners and highly defensible gateways. The siting of the castles was carefully thought out to use natural defences such as water and rock to the best advantage.

Caernarvon is a good example of a late 13th-Century castle built by Edward I. Its walls are up to 15 feet thick and remain virtually intact. There are other surviving examples of the same period at Caerphilly, Harlech and Conway.

Features of the Medieval castle were the *enceinte*, or outer wall, the moats or ditches surrounding the wall, often filled with water for additional defence (though this undoubtedly added to the dampness of life within the castle), the retractable drawbridge for crossing the moat, the barbican which was a double-fortified construction for protecting the gateway, and the portcullis made of oak plated with iron for lowering across the gateway. The walls were usually crenellated, or topped by battlements,

and the round towers and faces of the walls were punctuated by narrow loopholes from which the defenders could fire while offering the smallest possible target to the attacker.

Russia had 14th-Century fortified citadels, called kremlins, characterized by numerous towers. In India, emphasis was laid on outworks and heavily fortified gateways. Spikes often protruded from the great teak doors as additional defence against elephants used to act as living battering rams.

The appearance of cannon in the siege trains of the 15th Century gradually brought about the collapse of the Medieval castle, whose uprearing, vertical walls offered a prime and vulnerable target to the massive battering of the guns. Castles throughout Europe were rapidly reduced. Charles VII of France swept the English out of his country with a commanding siege train and his son pushed south through Italy with similar success. In the first half of the next century the Turks, under Suleiman I, battered fort after fort into submission throughout eastern Europe as they advanced threateningly toward Vienna, where eventually they were stopped.

For centuries fortifications had adapted themselves to the prevailing means of attack; it was time for them to do so again.

Above: From a painting of the Vodozvodnaya Tower of the Kremlin, in Moscow, as it used to appear.
Left: The imposing walls of Caernarvon Castle, one of the best preserved of Edward I's 13th-Century Welsh castles.
Right: The map shows the strategic positions of Edward I's castles in Wales.
Below: A ground plan of Conway Castle, another of Edward's fortifications, showing the typical round corner towers.

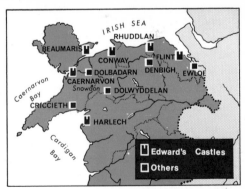

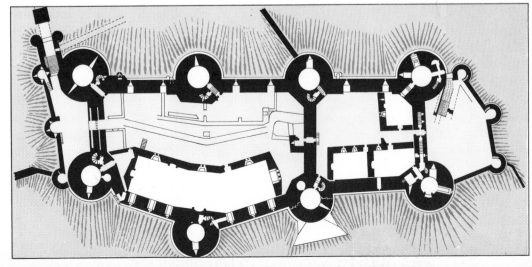

GUNPOWDER BREAKTHROUGH
Friar Bacon and Black Berthold

The use of gunpowder as an explosive charge to provide the power to fire missiles was the most influential innovation in the history of warfare. To this day the gun remains one of the most effective machines of war in a variety of shapes and sizes. But it is still not known who invented gunpowder nor who built the first gun.

The invention of gunpowder has been credited to the Chinese. There is no certainty of this. Experiments were made at an early date with oil, pitch and sulphur, but results were variable and often unstable. The Arabs may also have known about gunpowder in the early 13th Century A.D. But the first convincing report of its manufacture was by the Franciscan Friar, Roger Bacon, in the middle of the 13th Century. In a cyphered report, Bacon gave the formula for the correct mixture of saltpetre, charcoal and sulphur.

Bacon's claim to fame is certainly stronger than that of his rival, the German monk, Berthold Schwartz. Despite 'portraits' of him and a statue to his memory, as well as reports of his supposed invention of gunpowder, it is possible that Berthold was only a legend.

The first positive record of a gun is not until at least 60 years after Bacon's gunpowder formula. In 1326, permission was granted by the city council of Florence for a delivery of cannon balls and 'canones de metallo'. The first known illustration of a gun occurs in the same year. This is an illuminated manuscript written by Walter de Milemete in honour of King Edward III of England. In the illustration, a knight has just put a red hot iron to the touch-hole of a pot-bellied, vase-shaped cannon from whose mouth an arrow is being fired. This kind of cannon, because of its shape, was called a 'pot-de-fer'.

A year later there is evidence that Edward used guns in his first Scottish campaign; the Scots were using them in sieges soon afterwards. In 1346, we know that Edward used a small number of cannon in his victory over the French at the Battle of Crécy. The terrible noise of the cannon was feared as much as the destructive power of the cannon balls.

Stone Shot and Breeches

Early cannon, or bombards as they were often called – petarara and culverin were names for other types of cannon – were not necessarily cast. Staves of wood were laid lengthwise in a circular formation to form the barrel and were forced

Roger Bacon an English man

Above: Roger Bacon knew the formula for gunpowder. Right: A scene from the Battle of Rosebecque, from the Chronicles of the French Historian, Froissart. There are examples of early cannon in the scene itself and two shown in action below the battle.

together by rings of brass or iron. Sometimes the staves were made of iron as well. It was not a satisfactory method on the whole, as the gases from the explosion of the gunpowder tended to escape through the cracks.

Stone shot was used as an economy and convenience. It required less charge than iron; this also meant that there was a correspondingly reduced chance of the whole cannon blowing up, as frequently happened. But iron and lead shot came into use very quickly. Small shot was used against troops in the open.

Breech-loaders were introduced early in the history of guns. A trough was left at the rear of the gun into which was wedged a mug-shaped cylinder with a handle, complete with powder and shot. When the gun had been fired the cylinder was taken out and replaced by another that had already been prepared with powder and shot. By this means a fairly rapid rate of fire could be maintained; if enough cylinders, or chambers, were available, from 12–15 rounds could be fired in an hour.

Early carriages for the guns consisted merely of a great beam of timber, hollowed out so that the gun could lie snugly along its length. More elaborate carriages soon evolved to enable elevation and depression of the gun. This was particularly important for siege warfare, which was one of the immediate uses to which the new machines were put.

Bataille de Rosebecque.

Perrodin pinx.   Imp Fraillery   Daumont, chromolith.

THE GREAT CANNON
Characters from a Mighty Past

The use of cannon against castles and fortified city walls led very quickly to the construction of monster cannon, some of which are still intact today. Their dimensions and the statistics of their firepower and capabilities make formidable reading but can surely never recreate in the mind the terrifying effect on defenders to whom cannon of any kind were still a novelty.

Mad Margaret, or *Dulle Griet*, was one of the earliest, built about 1410 and still to be seen in the Belgian town of Ghent. Mad Margaret is over 16 feet long, weighs about 15 tons and has a bore of about 30 inches.

An even earlier cannon was Krimhild, which stood inside Nuremberg in 1388. It is reported that Krimhild's cannon balls had a range of 1,000 paces and could penetrate a wall that was six feet thick. Though not as large as Mad Margaret, something of Krimhild's size can be imagined when we know that 12 horses were needed to pull it and another 22 to draw up its ammunition and equipment.

Mons Meg is another famous cannon, built in Flanders in about 1470 and now at Edinburgh, in Scotland. Mons Meg is 13 feet long and weighs five tons. The cannon has a bore of almost 20 inches and could fire a stone shot of more than 300 pounds. With the right charge – and set at the right angle – the cannon could fire an iron ball over 1,400 yards and a stone ball nearly twice as far.

Mahomet's Dardanelles Monsters

Mahomet used several huge cannon at the siege of Constantinople in 1453, alongside his old-fashioned trebuchets. The strength of the fortification and the determination of the defence can be guessed at when it is remembered that, despite the battering of these cannon, the siege lasted for nearly two months. The 'Dardanelles Gun' now at the Tower of London, was built for Mahomet in the 1460s and is probably very like those used at the siege.

This gun was cast in bronze and weighs over 18 tons. It is 17 feet long, has a bore of 25 inches and fired a shot of approximately 800 pounds. An

unusual feature of the gun is that it was made in two pieces, which were screwed together. This was probably done for ease of transport.

It was fired experimentally almost 200 years after it was first built and the fragments of shot flew almost a mile to cross the Dardanelles. Even 350 years after their construction, Mahomet's siege guns were still in action: a British squadron was fired on in the Dardanelles and one ship received a hit from a 700-pound shot.

From an account of the construction of the guns we know that one was made in about 18 days and that it took 140 oxen and 200 men to haul each of the monsters into position against the walls of Constantinople. From that moment, Mahomet's 12 great cannon – a thirteenth burst early on – were each able to hurl about seven shots a day at the city defences for the duration of the siege.

The King of Cannon
One of the biggest cannon ever produced was in Russia, at the beginning of the 16th Century.

This was the massive 'King of Cannon', which had a bore of about 35 inches and a barrel of 17 feet. It could fire a stone ball weighing up to one ton.

At last the stubborn walls of cities that had been able to withstand sieges of months and intermittent attacks for years came crumbling down in only a few days. Some idea of the importance and charismatic value of these dominating monsters might be gained by reading C. S. Forester's *The Gun*, a story which was also made into a film. The story is set in more recent history and the gun itself is not as vast as some of the monsters in this chapter, but *The Gun* is a vivid account of the 'presence' which this outstanding and vital piece of artillery exerted over the soldiers who made use of it and among those against whom it was used.

Far left, top: Mons Meg, restored and remounted, stands at Edinburgh Castle. Far left, bottom: The Dardanelles Gun, built by the Turks in the 15th Century, now at the Tower of London. Below: The 17th-Century Tsar Pushka, or Emperor Cannon.

CANNON FOR EVERY PURPOSE
Making Good Use of the New Machine

As soon as the first guns appeared, inventive minds turned their attention to the novelty of the new machine and produced a proliferation of shapes and sizes, all with different purposes. Some of these never got further than the drawing board; illustrations and reports still exist even of these. It was one thing for an army to possess artillery but when both armies were in possession of the same advantage what was important was the manner in which the new machine was put to use and how its merits were exploited.

The first move was to combine several guns in one piece of artillery on the same gun-carriage.

These were usually fixed around a central block and each had its own touch-hole. One gun could be fired at a time or several together for added effect – and the effect could be startling. But the danger was as great for the artilleryman as it was for the enemy. While intending to fire only one of the guns, the gunner might explode the whole contraption in a self-destructive conflagration, much to the delight of the opposition.

Organ-guns, which were a variation of this multiple principle, had their barrels laid in a row, sometimes as many as ten side by side. Another form of organ-gun had three rows of

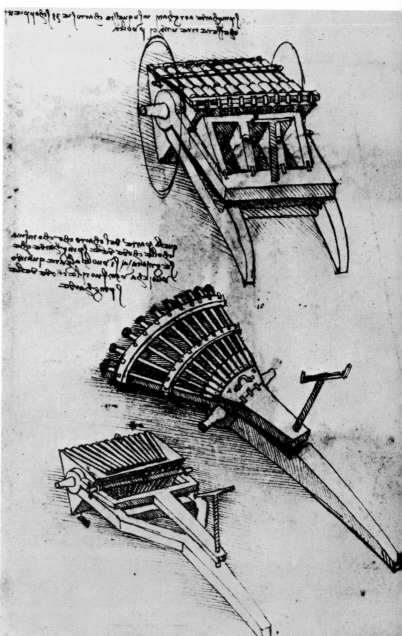

Above: Leonardo da Vinci's imaginative designs for organ-guns, with multiple fire-power. Left: An eight-barrelled gun carriage using a sledge base. Wheels would probably have stuck fast.

gun barrels laid side by side on the three sides of a triangular block that revolved in a frame so that each row aimed forward in turn and could be fired in rapid succession. Leonardo da Vinci made several drawings of organ-guns into which he incorporated a worm-screw system for elevating the contraption.

Ribaudequins and Shrimps

War chariots had been used before guns were invented but they took a new turn with the new circumstances. Immediately prior to the introduction of guns, the war chariot had consisted of a two-wheeled shield, pushed forward by soldiers, with pikes protruding through its face and loopholes provided for crossbow fire.

In the *ribaudequin*, the crossbows were replaced by small cannon, little more than tubes. We know that Edward III ordered a hundred of these ribaudequins to be prepared for his invasion of France, which led to the battle of Crécy. 150 years later, these basic war chariots were still in use in Germany.

Gun carts were a more sophisticated form of ribaudequins. Henry VIII of England tried to make use of them at the siege of Boulogne, in

1544. In this case the guns were given better cover. A conical nose to the gun cart culminated in one or more spikes. The guns themselves appeared through openings in the side of the cone. This type of gun cart was sometimes known as a 'shrimp'. Its bite was more than shrimp-like.

One illustration of a gun cart or ribaudequin from the 15th Century shows a horse in harness behind the gun pulling against the back of the frame in order to propel the whole machine forward. A shield protects the gunner and a vicious looking arrow projects forward of the gun barrel. Since the horse could hardly have been expected to attain much speed with the weight of the whole contraption, the arrow probably served the purpose of defence against charging cavalry rather than attack.

Zizka's Snakes

Another type of early gun cart or waggon was that used by the Protestant Hussites, led by John Zizka, against the Catholic Monarchists of Bohemia at the beginning of the 15th Century. Zizka organized wooden waggons, mounted with cannon, into circular formations. The waggons were covered and protected by thick boards, presenting a formidable defence, bristling with armament, against which the Bohemian cavalry, protected only by conventional armour, flung itself with self-destructive futility. Zizka's cannon were called 'snakes' and their bite was appropriately lethal.

The waggon barricade also served as a sanctuary for Zizka's infantry, who could make sudden sorties against the enemy and retreat as quickly behind the waggon train. The mobility of this train of artillery was one of its greatest assets. It amounted to a moveable fortress that could be set up on any prominent position ready for action at very short notice.

Three major innovations in early artillery warfare occurred during this century. Wheels were introduced on gun carriages, *trunnions* were developed and, in the middle of the century, bronze casting began to take the place of iron. Bronze could be cast more evenly and the cannon made with this metal were therefore less likely to explode under the shock of firing.

Trunnions were the pivots on either side of the cannon, cast at the same time as the cannon, and set slightly forward of the point of balance so that, when unsupported, the breech of the cannon came down and the muzzle was raised. The use of trunnions made it a great deal easier to elevate and depress the cannon in order to adjust the range and achieve maximum accuracy.

The Names of the Guns

The great siege cannon and giant bombards often had their own characterized names, such as

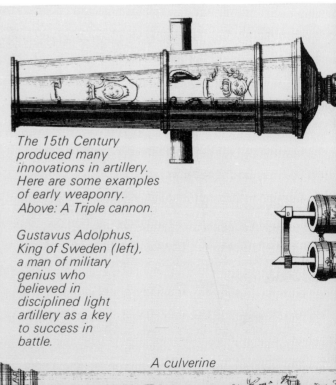

The 15th Century produced many innovations in artillery. Here are some examples of early weaponry. Above: A Triple cannon.

Gustavus Adolphus, King of Sweden (left), a man of military genius who believed in disciplined light artillery as a key to success in battle.

A culverine

Mons Meg, which has already been described, and the Katherine, a Tyrolean cannon cast in 1487, 12 feet long and inscribed with the verse, in German:

'My name is Katherine.

'Beware of my strength.

'I punish injustice.'

But apart from these special cases, the ordinary names for the various types of gun varied according to country, time and use, as did their shapes and sizes. Used initially as individual pieces of artillery, it was some time before any kind of standardization was applied to the guns that were being produced. And until that happened no rational organization of ammunition and equipment could be put into practice.

One of the enlightened commanders who contributed to this organization was the Emperor Maximilian, in about 1500. But still the proliferation of names and the variations in size and shot between countries and periods make for plenty of confusion. All the same, it gives an idea of the range of guns in use to name some of them and their capabilities.

The siege artillery of Maximilian consisted of demi or double cannon that fired shot of between 36 and 50 pounds, quarter cannon that fired 24–40-pound shot and basilisks or long culverins (from the French *couleuvre*, a snake) that fired shot from 12–24 pounds. The long basilisk had the accuracy needed for siege work. Basilisks bore names such as 'ibex', 'lizard' and 'crocodile', as well as 'wall-breaker' and 'beater'. Other guns were called 'nightingales' and, in the same refrain, 'singers'.

English cannon, later in the century, were divided into cannon royal or double cannon (in this case the double cannon seems to have been differentiated from the demi-cannon) that may have weighed up to 8,000 pounds and fired a ball of 60–70 pounds, whole cannon weighing 7,000 pounds and firing a ball of 40 pounds, and demi-cannon of 6,000 pounds, firing a 30-pound ball.

Culverins fired balls varying between 15 and 20 pounds and demi-culverins fired 10-to-12-pound balls. For field artillery there were sakers (from the French *sacre*, a sparrow hawk) that fired balls from six to seven pounds, minyons that fired three-to-four-pound balls, and falcons and falconets that fired respectively just over two-pound shots and one-pound shot.

But another inventory of artillery given a little earlier in Europe makes reference to falconets using four-to-five-pound shot and falcons using six-pound shot. A serpentine also fired a variable four-pound shot.

Among the less common pieces of artillery were quarter-culverins (half the fire-power of a demi-culverin), the small one-pounder serpentinelles, flankers, bastard cannons, perriers and

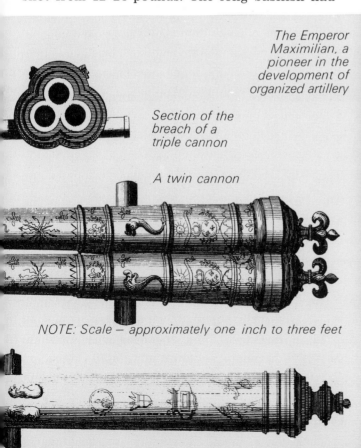

Section of the breach of a triple cannon

A twin cannon

NOTE: Scale – approximately one inch to three feet

The Emperor Maximilian, a pioneer in the development of organized artillery

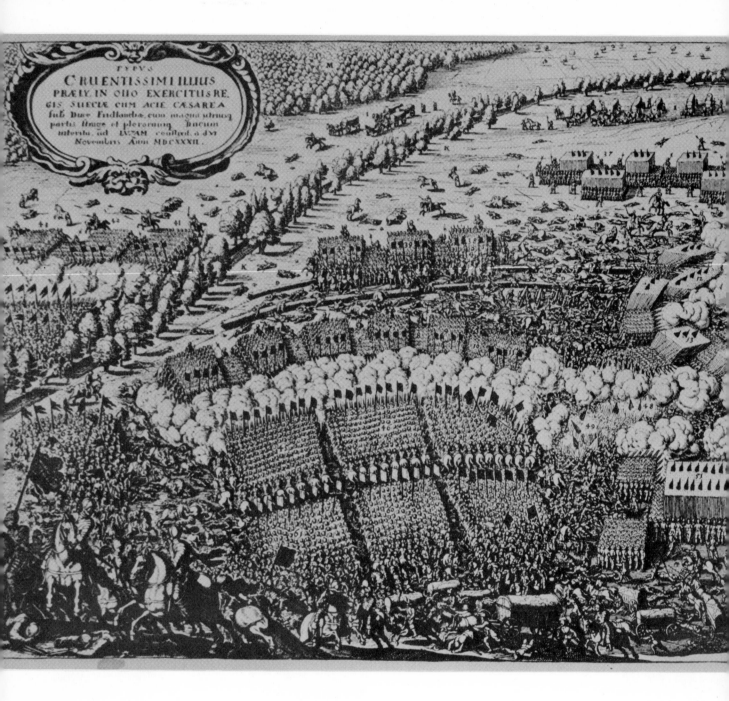

giant perriers (short-barrelled cannon), and the colourfully named 'murderers'. Mortars were also used in siege warfare but those machines are dealt with in the next chapter.

Field Artillery at Ravenna

By the 17th Century light field guns were in widespread use. Chief among the commanders who understood and put into practice the use of manoeuvrable field guns was the Swedish King Gustavus Adolphus, whose light three-pounder could be drawn by one horse or three men and saw action with great success during the 30 Years

War. In many ways, Gustavus's integration of field artillery with infantry and cavalry was the example for many later systems of integrated attack – systems that proved most effective.

But it was Maximilian who had really shown the value of concentrated artillery fire in the field as well as in siegework. The first large gatherings of artillery in the field took place during the Italian War of 1508–1516, in which Maximilian took part, together with English, French, Spanish, Venetian and Papal forces.

Massed ranks of infantry and the massed fire of the artillery played the major roles in these

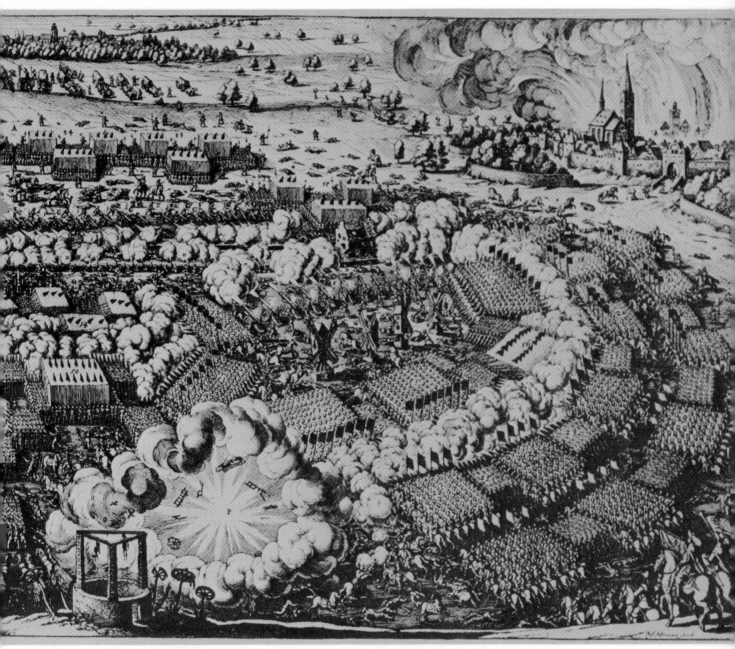

Lützen — The last battle fought by Gustavus Adolphus in the Thirty Years War. The great commander was killed while personally leading his troops into a battle which destroyed the Catholic army of Count Wallenstein.

campaigns. Artillery fire could tear apart the ranks of pikemen and halberdiers. But if the first volley failed to halt or turn the enemy's advance, time was against the guns. In the time that it took to reload the guns, the infantry could easily approach and overrun their positions.

An artillery duel opened the encounter between the French and Spanish at the Battle of Ravenna, in 1512. One report states that one Spanish cannon-ball knocked down almost 40 men. But a year later, at Novara, the cannon proved less effective. Possessing no artillery of their own and after sustaining a barrage of fire from the French artillery, Swiss mercenaries managed to capture all the French cannon in one daring attack. Good cause for celebration.

The French had their revenge two years later at the Battle of Marignano, when their substantial artillery decimated the Swiss troops. The combination of artillery and arquebus fire proved itself conclusively. 'The sky burst forth as if all the forces of the earth and heavens were preparing to swoop down', wrote one diarist. The hitherto invincible Swiss were routed, leaving 7,000 dead on the battlefield, mute evidence to the effectiveness of the new machine.

MORTARS: THE BARRAGE FROM ABOVE
Specialized Cannon

The mortar was a form of cannon specialized to lob shot over the wall of a besieged fortification or to deliver a plunging shot or spray of shots on an enemy from above. Mahomet used these machines to excellent effect in bombarding the Byzantine fleet in 1453.

The distinction between mortars and cannon was based on their angle of fire and the length of their barrels. Mortars, or short howitzers as they were sometimes known, fired in what was termed the upper register; that is, over 45 degrees. Cannon and guns fired in the lower register, below 45 degrees. The shorter barrel of the mortar, which was a variation on the early bombard, enabled a charge of shot to be spread over a wider area.

Leonardo's Bombard

In 1482, Leonardo da Vinci wrote that he had, 'a type of bombard that is extremely easy and convenient to transport and with which it is intended to shower a veritable hailstorm of small stones and whose smoke will strike the enemy with terror, causing great danger and confusion'. Very soon there were mortars in every train of artillery, although most armies seem to have restricted themselves at first to three or four of these high-angled machines.

Types and calibres of mortar differed as greatly as those of cannon. They continued to be used increasingly until, by the end of the 18th Century, it was generally accepted that the length of a mortar should be approximately one and a half to a maximum of two times its calibre. Mortars were loaded from the muzzle and their trunnions were usually at the extreme base, behind the touch-hole, in order to facilitate a steep angle of fire. Instead of wheeled carriages, flat-based beds were used for supporting the mortar, which was transported on a specially designed waggon, whereas the howitzer, apart from being longer, was generally transported on a conventional gun carriage and its trunnions were usually placed just off-centre.

One of the more popular mortars was the powerful 10-inch mortar that could fire a shot up to 1,500 yards. Once again, distances and size varied greatly. An eight-inch mortar was also commonly used. And as well as single shot and multiple shot, bombs filled with gunpowder were fused to explode after a set time. The accuracy of this timing could not be counted on, nor could the gunner's estimation of the range. Illustrations of the strategic deployment of troops, showing mortars firing over their heads at the enemy toward whom they are advancing, look dangerous. Many shots must have landed accidentally among friends as well as enemies.

Shrapnel and Exploding Shells

The danger to troops was increased when bombs were timed to burst over the heads of the enemy, adding an increased element of fear to the physical threat. To achieve this effect successfully against the intended target made considerable demands on the accuracy of the gunners.

It was Lieutenant Shrapnel of the British army who invented the famous shell case that bears his name. The case was hollow, fitted with small shot and a fuse light enough to break up the case without dispersing the shot, which continued in the direction in which it had been aimed. Although Shrapnel introduced his idea in the 1780s, it was not used by the British until the Napoleonic wars.

Top right: A sketch by Leonardo, showing a design for elevating a mortar on a toothed arc.
Bottom right: Another Leonardo sketch showing the trajectories of mortar bombs used against a fortress and giving blanket coverage.
Below: Two types of bombard, or mortar, set on flat-based beds, from an engraving published in 1575. The one on the left has its trunnions at the base of the barrel, that on the right has central trunnions. The T-shape and angle lying by the mortar bomb are used for aiming the mortar.

ASPECTS OF THE CANNON
Aiming and Firing

The arrival of the gun introduced a new field of science to warfare and the strategy of sieges. Powder and shot, breech carriage, wadding and rammer – these were all important to the gunner; so were his methods of aiming. Without an understanding of technique, the machine was useless.

To determine the angle of elevation for his gun and thereby take effective aim, the gunner used a quadrant, a right angle piece of metal with a graded curve along the third side. The gunner held the quadrant so that one arm sighted along the barrel of the gun and a plumb line attached to the inside angle of the two arms dropped down past the graded curve. By reading off the graded mark against which the plumb line lay, and referring to his chart, the gunner could estimate the trajectory of his shot. It was an Italian, Niccolo Fontana, who died in 1557, who first laid down mathematical rules for the trajectories of guns.

In siege warfare different methods of fire were used against various types of defence. For instance, against a square tower, cannon were aimed from an angle against the corners of the fortification in order to dislodge the corner stones. A circular tower could more easily be breached by concentrating the fire on one point until, repeatedly weakened and cracked, the whole tower was inevitably brought down. Manuals and diagrams of instruction spread quickly during the 16th Century.

Casting the Gun

Advances were soon made in the casting of the guns so that the gunner could apply his knowledge of technique to a machine on which he could at least rely to fire as expected. The method of casting guns in the 18th Century was a slow and painstaking job but the guns that were produced, and many of which survive, bear excellent testimony to the care and precision that went into their production.

A wooden core resting on two trestles was covered by straw or rope wound tightly round and hammered down for increased firmness. This was then covered by a layer of fine clay, brickdust and even grease to hold it together. As this mould was revolved on the trestles, it was smoothed and shaped; trunnions were added, as well as all the decorations that would eventually show on the gun itself. As the clay was applied it was carefully dried to avoid cracking.

The quadrant facilitated accurate fire.

This replica of the gun was then covered with *the cope* – several more thin and carefully dried layers of clay – which was finally secured by straps of iron in order to hold it firmly together. This cope was sometimes made in sections which were taken apart in order to extract the mould and core and then secured together again by the straps. Alternatively, the core and mould were carefully drawn out from the entire cope.

The next stage was to pour the molten metal into the cope. If the bore of the barrel was to be drilled out after casting, then the metal was

poured in to fill the whole cavity within the cope; if not, then a narrow core was carefully fitted into place and locked at either end to form the bore. This was first greased for ease of removal after the casting process.

In the case of the drilling technique, which was more advanced, the bore was drilled either vertically or horizontally. Vertically, the cannon was placed muzzle down on a revolving drill so that its own weight helped to drive the drill up through its length. In the horizontal position, which became the more popular, the drill was usually fixed and driven round by horsepower (later, by steampower), while the cannon was moved forward against the drill. It was in fact possible to move the drill forward against the stationary cannon.

Finally, the decorations were polished up and the cannon was weighed and tested to ensure that it did not crack on the first shot. Those that failed the test, as well as those that cracked or were destroyed in battle, could always be melted down again for re-use – the manufacture of yet another machine for yet another battle.

THE VAUBAN FORT
A Scientific Art

The Vauban fort was the medieval castle's answer to the challenge of the guns but the remarkable achievement of Sebastian de Vauban was that he mastered the technique not only of constructing modern fortifications against siege gunfire but of overcoming his own fortresses. He reduced warfare to a scientific art, whose outcome, so far as he was concerned, was decided in advance. He was the greatest military engineer of his generation and his influence continued long after his death. His 'systems' of fortification and siege-craft were studied and imitated for more than a century.

Vauban accompanied the French King Louis XIV on almost all his campaigns throughout the second half of the 17th Century. During this time he has been credited with constructing or rebuilding over 150 fortresses. The famous star-shaped fortress that he designed made maximum use of a low profile against the attacking guns, an ingenious system of crossfire against the attack, and depth of defence.

Digging Down for Defence

Instead of building *up* for defence, Vauban's reaction was to dig *down*. Defenders were protected by covered ways, parapets and low ramparts of earth and stone which helped to deflect the shot of the attackers over the heads of those within the defensive ditch. Bastions were added projecting out from the fortress to form the star shape and to enable the fire of the defending guns to overlap each other and so to cover completely any approach.

Vauban designed fortresses at Strasbourg, Luxemberg and Landau, among many other places. One of his most famous fortresses was at Neuf-Brisach.

His complementary achievement was specifically designed to reduce these same star-shaped fortresses and can be seen both as an indication of their strength – that such craft was required to overcome them – and their weakness – that the techniques of their destruction could be repeated with confidence time and time again, against fortress after fortress.

Low-profile Attack

In the same way that the defence relied on a low profile, so did the attack. Siege artillery was placed round the fortress under attack so that its fire covered every facet of the bastions. These

Sebastian de Vauban, Marshall of France.

artillery positions were linked by trenches sometimes 15–20 feet wide and three to four feet deep. This first 'parallel', as it was called, was usually at the extreme range of the guns; that was about 600–700 yards.

Under cover of the artillery, zig-zag trenches were dug toward the fortress, at a rate of about 50 yards a day under reasonable conditions. Along these 'saps', the attackers could advance without fear of receiving the full force of the defenders' fire down a straight trench. Half way to the fortress, a second parallel was dug. Artillery was brought forward and the bombardment became hotter from closer range.

Attack and defence took the form of constant bombardment until, as further saps approached the first line of defence, the combat often broke up into sorties and hand-to-hand fighting for possession of the guns. At handgun range the attackers prepared for the final onslaught. Foreseeing the inevitability of defeat, a fortress might often be persuaded to surrender before the final stage, on the promise of reasonable treatment by the victors. Such a code of behaviour was encouraged by Vauban whenever possible.

Vauban achieved his first success with this method of parallel assault against Maestricht in 1673. It fell after 13 days. But he had already achieved siege successes of one kind or another in the war of the Spanish Fronde – Stenay fell after 33 days in 1654; Gravelines fell four years later; in the Dutch wars he achieved successes against Tournai, Douai and Lille.

After these successes, the fortress became a tactic to delay an enemy, not to stop him. Vauban's victory against himself was complete.

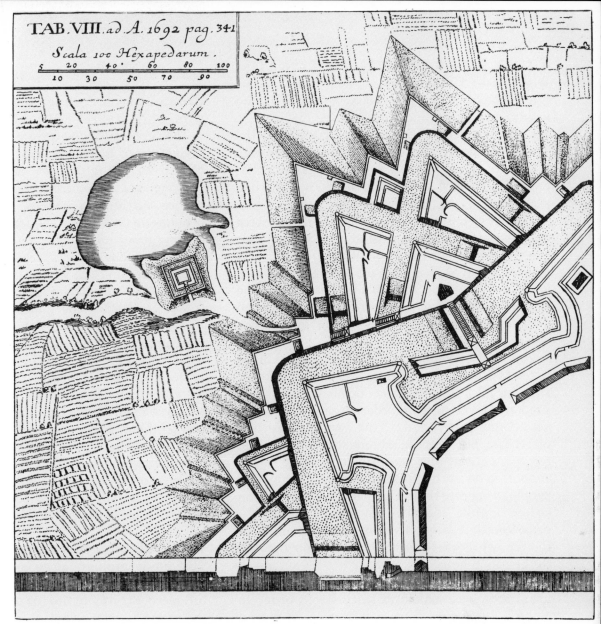

TAB. VIII. ad. A. 1692 pag. 341

Scala 100 Hexapedarum.

5   20   40.   60   80   100
  10   30   50   70   90

Right: The Ground plan for a Vauban fortification, showing part of the complex star-shaped defence system, which allowed the fields of fire from the fortress to overlap. A cross-section of the elevation of the fortress is keyed in to the plan along the bottom of the print.

Below: A painting of the Fortress of Luxembourg today. A fine example of a naturally fortified site.

FROM BOMBARDELLI TO FLINTLOCK
Miniature Cannon

Once the cannon had been recognized and established as the most destructive machine so far encountered in the history of warfare, the next step clearly was to arm the foot-soldier with a smaller version of this device – a cannon that could be carried easily and used in a flexible situation.

The first handguns developed directly from early cannon. They consisted of a simple iron tube, or breech, with a touch-hole. After early attempts proved that the tube became too hot to hold once a round or two had been fired, the breech was fitted with a wooden handle, called a tiller, fixed by iron straps or slotted into the end of the breech.

One of the earliest references to handguns is in the town records of Perugia, in Italy. We know that in 1364 five hundred 'bombardelli', to be fired by the hand, were ordered; each was to be about nine inches long. This sounds more like pistol size, but many handguns were clumsy and heavy contraptions, sometimes needing to be supported on the ground and often requiring two people to operate them. One man held the weapon either against his chest or under his arm – occasionally against his shoulder – and aimed at the foe, while the other applied the slow match to the touch-hole.

The slow match consisted of a string of woven hemp that was soaked in saltpetre in order to make it burn more slowly. This was, in fact, a sophisticated method of firing the priming powder that only developed at the end of the 14th Century and replaced the awkward method of heating a piece of wire over a convenient fire (if there was such a thing) and then applying the wire, while still red-hot, to the pan.

The first handguns were a strange and varied collection of machines, motley cross-breeds intended for use not merely as guns, which were far too novel to be considered in any way reliable, but as battle axes, maces, daggers, clubs and other more traditionally effective devices in case of emergency and in the heat of battle when the soldier's mechanical expertise failed him.

This combination within the same machine of the gun and a traditional striking weapon continued long after the gun itself had developed into an efficient and thoroughly dependable contraption; the bayonet was of course a similar, if more rational, form of this combination.

Despite its clumsiness, the handgun proved its worth immediately. The knight's armour, as we have seen, until then only vulnerable to the powerful bolt of the crossbow and the searching aim of the longbow, was no proof against bullets from handguns with calibres varying from half an inch to almost two inches; no proof, that was, so long as the soldier who operated the gun could achieve a hit, which was never certain.

The Problems of Taking Aim

The single gunner, quite apart from knowing little or nothing about ballistics, had both hands full merely trying to fire his contraption without the added but somewhat necessary complication of trying to aim at his target. Holding the gun with one hand, the gunner had to blow on the slow match until it glowed and then apply it carefully to the touch-hole, by which time the

Left: From a painting by Glockenthon of the Emperor Maximilian I's guns. The men are firing a hand cannon of about 1505.
Right: Two early and unusual multi-barrel guns from Maximilian's Arsenal of Tyrol: a four-cornered gun and a triple-barrel matchlock.

March with your rest in your hand.

March, and with your Musket carry your rest.

Unshoulder your Musket.

Guard, blow and open your pan.

Poize your Musket

Join your rest to your Musket.

Take forth your Match.

Dismount your musket.

Uncoc...

Blow off your coal.

Cock your Match.

Try your Match.

Clear your pan.

Prin...

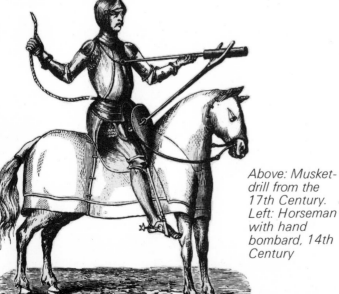

Above: Musket-drill from the 17th Century. Left: Horseman with hand bombard, 14th Century

priming powder had probably blown away. Sometimes a strap was provided on the end of the tiller, which went round the gunner's neck to steady his aim; later, a regular support was part of his equipment.

What was needed was a method of igniting the powder that would leave the gunner with a hand free to steady his weapon and take more telling aim. This was provided, in about 1480, by the introduction of the serpentine, an S-shaped piece of metal fixed to the side of the gun. The slow match was held in one end of the serpentine and brought down on to the touch-hole when the lower end of the 'S' – the trigger – was pulled.

This invention, simple at first, more complex and more efficient as further sophistications were

Give Fire.

Cast of your loose powder.

Blow of your loose powder.

Cast about your Musket.

Return your match.

Trail your rest.

Open your Charge.

Charge your Musket.

Shut your pan.

Draw forth your scouring Stick.

Shorten your scouring Stick.

Put in your Bullet & Ram home.

added, transformed the infantry gunner from a fringe benefit to a lethal and increasingly vital facet of the battle scene.

Early handguns, or arquebus, were first used in an integrated system of infantry at the beginning of the 16th Century, when they began to replace bowmen interspersed between ranks of pikemen and swordsmen. Hopefully, what the arquebus failed to stop the pikes would hold off while the arquebus reloaded.

The variety of early handguns closely paralleled the variety of early cannon. There was even a hand mortar. And in the same way that experiments were made to produce multiple guns, so multiple handguns appeared. Similarly, as spears had sometimes been reversible, so there were

reversible handguns, though this style did not survive long. Every innovation had to be experimented with from every possible angle in order fully to explore its potential.

The Arquebus

There were several stages in the development of the gun, each clearly discernible as the machine became increasingly efficient. Over a period of 300 years various mechanisms were invented for firing the handgun, each of which added to the gunner's reliability, accuracy and effectiveness, and each of which in turn produced a new machine with new capabilities.

The matchlock, or serpentine fitting, was, as we have seen, the first to enable the gunner to

take any reasonable kind of aim. This type of gun had a variety of names, the best known of which was probably 'arquebus'. It is possible that the word came from the Italian *arca bousa*, which means the 'bow with a mouth', for the stock of the crossbow was the nearest parallel to this new device that most soldiers had seen. The 'hackbutt' was a heavier form of arquebus, with a hook on its underside which was used to balance the gun against a stone wall or similar support.

The arquebus weighed anything up to 25 pounds and probably fired a one ounce ball about 100 yards. At close range, the ball could penetrate conventional armour of the early 16th Century with little difficulty.

The Wheel-lock and Pistol

Although modifications were made to the matchlock, there was still a tendency for the slow match to blow out in the wind and a likelihood that if it did not then its burning would give away the whereabouts of the gunner. The wheel-lock, which was invented about 1500, solved both these problems.

The wheel-lock worked by friction, rather like a cigarette lighter. A spark was produced to fire the priming powder when a piece of iron pyrites, a common mineral, struck down against a steel wheel with a milled edge. The pyrites was held

Above: An arquebusier of 1608 charges his weapon. He will then ram home the powder and shot before taking up his stance for firing.
Below: A beautifully decorated German wheel-lock petronel of about 1590, now in the Tower of London, England.

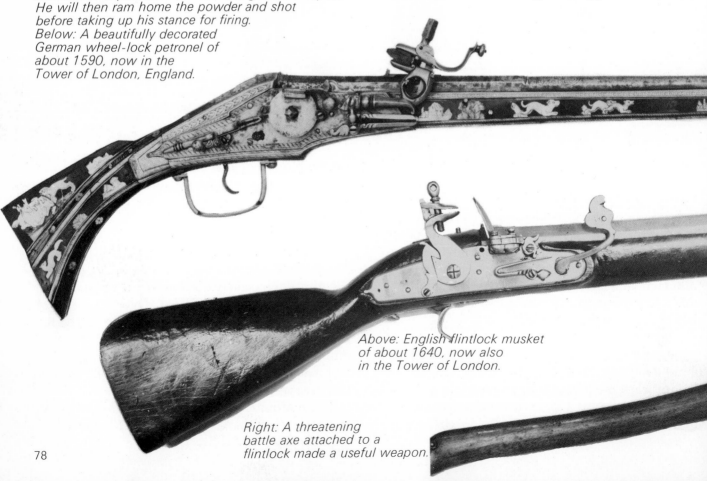

Above: English flintlock musket of about 1640, now also in the Tower of London.

Right: A threatening battle axe attached to a flintlock made a useful weapon.

78

in the 'dogshead' or 'cock' and the wheel was made to revolve by means of a spring wound up by a handle at the side of the gun. The trigger actuated the spring. You can see from the illustration that the cock was similar in concept to the serpentine that had held the slow match of the arquebus.

One of the earliest forms of friction lock, a great deal earlier than the wheel-lock, was the so-called Monk's gun, which was made in Germany, possibly in the second half of the 15th Century. In this device, the gunner drew out a lever which rubbed a serrated edge along a piece of iron pyrites, similar to the system in the wheel-lock.

The great advantage of the wheel-lock was that it could be fitted to a compact gun. Thus the pistol first appeared at the beginning of the 15th Century. Soldiers on horseback, unable to use the arquebus because it required two hands to fire, carried guns for the first time. Primed before battle, these pistols were often multi-barrelled, enabling the cavalryman to exert a considerable barrage of fire power as he passed close to the enemy before retiring to reload or before charging into the midst of the enemy with sword or mace.

Organized cavalry, armed with pistols, were used in 1544 by Germans attacking the French in Champagne. A hundred years later short

firearms with wheel-locks were being used in the English Civil War along with old matchlocks, although by that time the flintlock had been invented. The change-over from one type of gun to another always occurred over a long period of time. A sudden switch was too expensive.

The Snapping Hen
The flintlock appeared in about 1630, possibly in France, and survived for 200 years. But an earlier form of flintlock, called the snaphaunce, dates from about 1530. The word 'snaphaunce' possibly comes from 'snap haan', which meant 'snapping' or 'pecking' hen in Flemish.

In these two guns the cock, holding a piece of flint, struck down against a steel above the pan, where the powder was. As the steel was struck, it moved up and away from the pan, exposing the powder to the spark. In the snaphaunce there was a separate pan cover, which also moved back as the steel was struck. The flintlock was simplified by combining steel and pancover.

The matchlock was not generally abolished until the 18th Century. William II re-armed the British army with flintlocks in about 1700. The famous Brown Bess flintlock musket appeared at the beginning of the 18th Century. Flintlocks were used by almost all soldiers fighting in the Napoleonic wars.

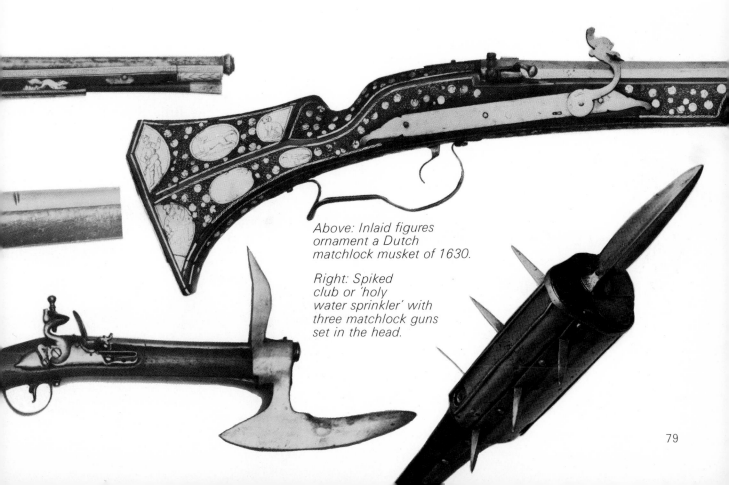

Above: Inlaid figures ornament a Dutch matchlock musket of 1630.

Right: Spiked club or 'holy water sprinkler' with three matchlock guns set in the head.

THE MODERN RIFLE TAKES SHAPE
Bayonets and Skilful Tactics

The word 'bayonet' comes from Bayonne in France, a place that had a reputation for its knives. The first bayonet appeared in about 1640, when a group of infantrymen stuck their knives into the muzzles of their guns and charged the enemy. The usefulness of this innovation was seen at once. Until then only the long and somewhat unwieldy pike had protected the infantryman as he reloaded his gun; with the bayonet he had his own simple defence. In 1647, a French Infantry Commander (also from Bayonne) ordered a quantity of short, round-handled swords from the town, and issued them to his musketeers. These were the first real bayonets.

Subsequent early bayonets were called 'plug' bayonets. A short, pointed, broad-based blade with a cross-guard and a wooden handle was shoved into the mouth of the musket when it was no longer needed. This meant, of course, that the gun itself could not be used simultaneously, a problem that was overcome by Sebastian Vauban, famous for his fortresses, who introduced the 'ring' bayonet, a tube attachment fitted with a triangular tapering blade – the tube slipped over the end of the gun and was help in place by a catch or spring clip.

Quicker to produce in an emergency was the 'spring' bayonet, introduced in the second half of the 18th Century. In this case the bayonet was permanently fixed to the gun but folded back along the barrel. When required it could be released to swing forward on a spring. Sometimes even pistols were fitted with these bayonets.

Marlborough made good use of the ring bayonet in his campaign against the French in the early years of the 18th Century. By this method he could raise the number of his musketeers at the expense of his pikemen and so bring more firepower to bear on the enemy. His victories at Blenheim, Oudenarde and Malplaquet, among others, bear witness to his skilful use of the efficient military machine at his disposal—victories that Britain was thankful for.

Pennsylvania Accuracy

The technique of rifling was known from an early stage in the making of guns but it was difficult to put into practice. In theory, if the ball was made to spin as it left the barrel, its accuracy would be greatly increased. The same theory had even been applied to arrows.

To make the ball spin, delicate spiralling grooves had to be cut on the inside surface of the barrel. This was a long job to be done by hand. But it was successfully achieved by many North American settlers in the middle of the 18th Century, who produced the lethal and renownedly accurate Pennsylvania or Kentucky rifle.

The skill that went into the construction of this rifle was brought over from Europe by German immigrants. At first used for hunting game, it was soon found to be equally effective against Indians. During the American War of Independence its long-barrelled accuracy accounted for the death of many British soldiers.

The history of rifling in fact goes back to the 15th or early 16th Century and soldiers began using them in the 17th Century. A rifled carbine was the armament of at least some of the French cavalry regiments before 1680, and the Baker rifle was used by the Rifle Brigade during the Napoleonic Wars.

Right: Half stock of the long-barrelled and lethally accurate Kentucky rifle.

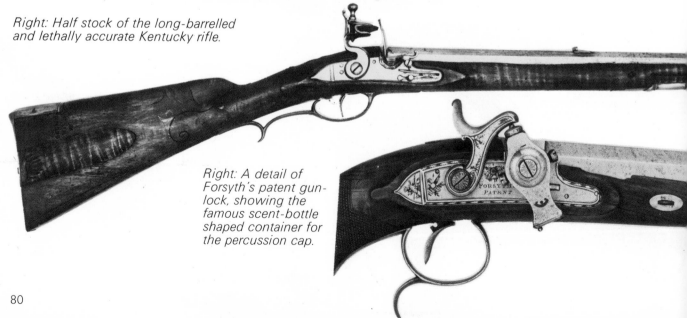

Right: A detail of Forsyth's patent gun-lock, showing the famous scent-bottle shaped container for the percussion cap.

From Scent Bottle to Needle Gun

The Pennsylvania rifle still made use of the flint-lock. A new device for firing a gun was introduced by the Reverend Alexander Forsyth, in 1805 and put into use about 10 years later. The percussion cap was a big step forward.

The drawback to the flintlock lay chiefly in the delay between pulling the trigger and firing the shot. This was called the 'hangfire' and was caused by the necessity, before the powder itself was ignited, to ignite the priming. Something of a chemist, Forsyth applied his knowledge to the firing mechanism of the rifle. He knew that a group of chemicals called fulminates would explode on impact. A few crystals placed in his famous 'scent bottle' shaped container exploded immediately on being struck by the hammer. This explosion ignited the main charge. The result was quicker than the flintlock and more reliable; it was later improved by the introduction of a copper percussion cap.

Captain Patrick Ferguson of the British army invented a breech-loading rifle in 1776. Attempts of a similar nature had even been made early in the 16th Century. But Ferguson's idea was not taken up. Only 100 of his rifles were supplied to the British army. It was left to the Prussians, in 1841, first to adopt a reliable breech-loader. In 1866, the French adopted the Chassepôt and in 1871, the British adopted the Martini-Henry rifle.

The Prussian breech-loader was the Von Dreyse needle gun, designed in 1827. A self-contained cartridge – including ball, powder and percussion compound – was fitted into the bore through a bolt-action breech. The percussion fulminate exploded the powder when the fulminate itself was struck by a long, thin, spring-operated needle. This needle was pulled back when the rifle was cocked and released when the trigger was pulled, so that it shot forward to pierce the cartridge cover. There was only one disadvantage: the delicate needle had an unsatisfactory tendency to snap off.

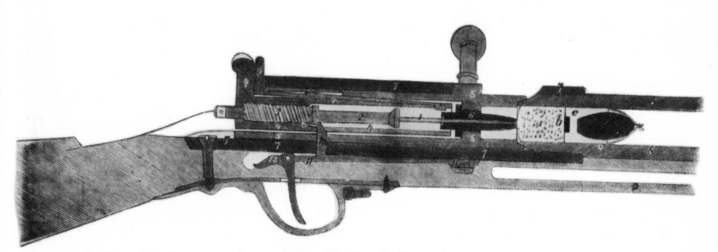

Above: Mechanism of the Dreyse needle-gun. Below: The French Chassepôt.

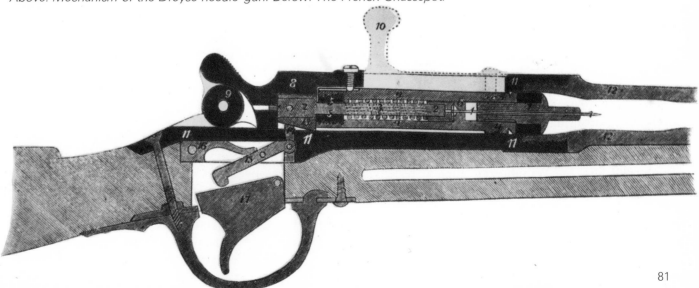

Above: Texas rangers armed with Winchester repeating rifles and revolvers, and equipped with ammunition belts.

Right: Indians as well as Rangers coveted the Winchester. Geronimo, on the right, with three warriors in 1886; the two on the left have Winchesters. Chappo, second from left, is Geronimo's son.

The Winchester and the West

This famous American rifle aptly deserved its title, 'The gun that won the West'. Its repeater action was operated by a lever connected to the trigger guard, in much the same way as the 'Henry' – another famous repeater operated. The Winchester with a brass frame was introduced in 1866 by the Winchester Repeating Arms Corporation, formed, strangely, by a shirt manufacturer, Oliver Winchester.

The magazine contained a spring. When the trigger guard was pulled down, the cartridge was pushed out of the magazine and fed into the breech as the guard was brought up again. Empty cases were ejected as the guard was moved. The rapid fire made possible by the repeater assured its success: to match the opposition, everyone wanted a Winchester.

It was used not only in the West but by the Turks as well. In 1884, the Germans introduced a magazine rifle for their army, to be followed by the French and Austrians in 1886 and then by the British only another two years later.

A Rifle for Two World Wars

Although the Prussian army had been quick to adopt the Von Dreyse needle gun, the modern British army dithered over adopting any specific rifle for general use. If the infantry were to be issued with a universal machine (if the army, that meant, was to go to the expense of equipping the infantry with a specific machine) then the army wanted to make sure that the machine was reliable. No one intended to waste money.

By the end of the 1880s the army settled on the bolt-action, magazine loaded Lee Metford, which held five rounds of ·303 inch ammunition. This had been designed by James Lee. Some modifications were made at the Royal Small Arms Factory at Enfield, which resulted in the Lee-Enfield. Further modifications included shortening the gun and extending the magazine to hold 10 rounds.

This Lee-Enfield ·303 was introduced in 1895 and used by the British infantry in both World Wars, a record of durability and reliability that must rank it as a very successful war machine.

RAPID FIRE FROM THE REVOLVER
The Pepperbox Machine

The pistol was a convenient machine to fire with one hand. At first its mechanical development largely followed the lines of the handgun. Wheel-lock mechanisms were succeeded by flint-locks and double-barrelled and multi-barrelled weapons were also popular. However, the flint-lock still took time – and two hands – to reload. It was the introduction of the percussion cap that gave the pistol the chance to show its true worth and operate with efficiency.

The revolver differed from the early pistol in that it had a 'revolving' chamber into which several bullets could be fitted and fired in succession. Although an American, Elisha Collier, had produced a flintlock revolver of a kind in 1820, and there had been attempts at revolver construction as early as the 16th Century. it was the metallic percussion mechanism that first enabled efficient revolvers to be produced.

By the middle of the 19th Century, the pepperbox revolver had appeared. This had a solid metal barrel with five or six bores which were either revolved by hand or, in the more sophisticated versions, revolved by the action of pulling back the trigger. The pepperbox was barrel-heavy and not very accurate; it was best used in self-

Above: The original wooden model for Colt's first revolver. Right: Samuel Colt, whose revolvers were used all over the world

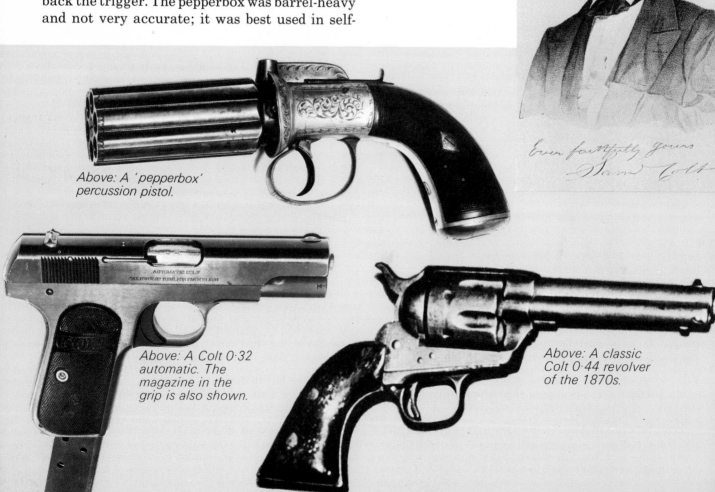

Above: A 'pepperbox' percussion pistol.

Above: A Colt 0·32 automatic. The magazine in the grip is also shown.

Above: A classic Colt 0·44 revolver of the 1870s.

defence. Even so, there were dangers: one barrel might well ignite the others, with alarming results similar to those with early firearms.

The Legend of Samuel Colt

The most famous revolver and the first that was really simple and efficient was made by Samuel Colt, born in Connecticut in 1814. Colt was fascinated by guns from an early age. During a voyage as midshipman in the brig *Corlo*, when he was 16, he carved out of wood a model of a six-chambered, single-barrelled revolver. When his father helped him to get a working model of the revolver made, the prototype blew up on the first shot.

The setback did not last long. Colt soon had a patent out and was in production. His revolvers were 'single action': as the hammer was pulled back, or cocked, with the thumb, the cylinder automatically rotated and was locked into position. Pressure on the trigger released the hammer. Two of Colt's most famous models were the Navy Colt, bought in large quantities by the British for use in the Crimean War, and the Frontier Colt, which went into production after his death.

Colt's revolvers were used in the Mexican War and the American Civil War; they became part of the legend of the great gold rushes; they endured in a modified form into the 20th Century. The name of Colt became a symbol for the age of American mid-west expansion.

Rivals to the Colt

When Colt came to England in 1851 to manufacture his revolvers, he met a rival in the form of Robert Adams, who had produced a double-action revolver. This was self-cocking: when a certain pressure was applied to the trigger, the cylinder automatically rotated and the hammer cocked; with additional pressure, the hammer fell forward and the revolver fired.

The Tranter revolver improved on the Adams by incorporating a double trigger. Pressure on the lower trigger cocked the gun and revolved the cylinder; pressure on the upper trigger, within the guard, fired the gun.

Another famous name in revolvers was Webley. The short, stocky, 'British Bulldog' saw service with the British army all over the world, during the First World War and even into the Second. It was a convenient machine that won the respect of all who used it, as well as the respect of those against whom it was used.

Above and right: A revolver from the Crimean War, with cleaning and cap-making equipment.

Above: A Colt 0.38 revolver.

Above: Smith and Wesson 0.38 automatic.

MACHINE GUNS FOR MASSACRE

Above: Gatling 0·65 inch calibre machine gun made by Armstrong. Below: Gardner single-barrelled 0·45 inch calibre machine gun.

Left: Puckle machine gun with square shot magazine, and spare magazine on the ground.

MACHINE GUNS FOR MASSACRE
Square Shot for Heathens

Since the invention of the gun, everyone's idea had been to make it fire faster, but the modern automatic machine gun took a long time to evolve. The mid-14th-Century organ guns were among the first quick-firers, but one of the first recognisable machine guns – a long way ahead of parallel designs – was that invented in 1718 by James Puckle. It was said to have fired 63 shots in seven minutes – in a rainstorm!

Puckle's patent was for a 'portable gun or machine called a defence'. There was a single barrel and a chamber of six or more cylinders, ignited by flintlock. A handle at the rear turned the cylinders and moved forward on a thread to lock each firmly into position. Two magazines were provided, one for round shot against 'Christians' and one for square shot against 'Heathens' or Turks. In his advertisement, Puckle stated that:

'Defending King George, your Country and
    Lawes
Is Defending Yourselves and Protestant
    Cause.'

Although Puckle formed a company to promote his gun, it never became popular; in fact it saw virtually no action. But manually operated machine guns reappeared over 140 years later, during the American Civil War, where they caused tremendous slaughter.

Civil War Suicide

Several types of machine gun appeared, the first of which, designed by an American called Williams, was initiated at the Battle of Fair Oaks, in 1862. The most famous was the Gatling, which came into use toward the end of the war. Richard Gatling was a planter, who lived in North Carolina. He patented his first quick-firing gun in 1862 and three years later obtained another patent. The following year his machine was officially adopted by the army.

A crank, or handle, was still used to turn the cylinders, which contained from six to ten barrels. The magazine with the cartridges was a hopper fixed above the gun so that the force of gravity dropped the cartridges into the magazine as the empty chambers came round. Each chamber fired in succession at a certain point, after which the case was automatically ejected as the crank continued to turn.

Early Gatlings could fire about 300 rounds per minute, although some of the ten-barrel models

The Puckle Gun and some of its equipment. The Magazine for round bullets is shown immediately below the front of the barrel, the one for square shot is shown below that. The tongs on the right are a mould for bullets.

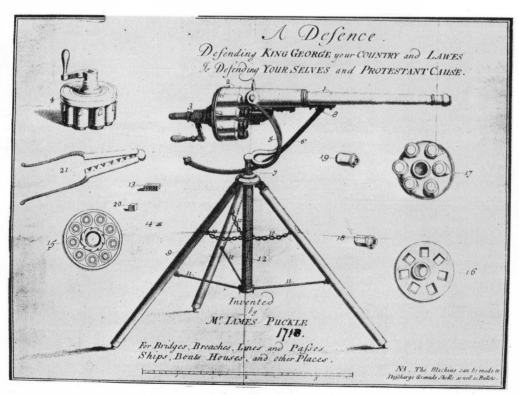

could fire up to 600 rounds. The effect of this kind of barrage on massed troops accustomed only to the rate of fire of the ordinary rifle may be imagined in both physical and psychological terms. Men fell and their courage faltered.

Grant's bloody victories in the latter part of the Civil War must have seemed suicidal to those involved on both sides. During the summer of 1864, over 80,000 men were killed in the two armies during six weeks fighting – slaughter on a scale that had never been encountered before. The Gatling was bought by the British for trials in 1870 and used with devastating effect in the Zulu wars in South Africa.

From the Mitrailleuse to the Maxim

It was in the Franco-Prussian war of 1870 that another, and earlier, machine gun proved itself. This was the French mitrailleuse. In French, *mitraille* meant 'grapeshot' and the Montigny mitrailleuse, invented in 1851, delivered a rate of fire of approximately 175 rounds per minute, though some said that this could go as high as 444 rpm – more destructive and a good deal more accurate than old-style grapeshot.

The Montigny had several barrels, which were mounted on a field gun carriage. The magazine consisted of a metal plate, perforated to contain a number of cartridges, that slotted into the breech block. When this was closed, the cartridges fitted into the barrels, which were fired in succession by the usual method of rotating a handle. Well over 100 shots per minute could be fired, with an effective range of nearly 1,000 yards.

Despite their mitrailleuse, the French had not mastered the techniques of tactical machine gun warfare. The Prussians were able to use their needle gun to much greater advantage.

Various other machine guns were tried out at this time, all with cranking handles. Among these was the Gardner, which was used for a while by the British navy to replace the Gatling. But the Gardner was inferior to the Nordenfelt, which appeared during the 1870s. The Gardner fired just over 100 shots per minute; the Nordenfelt ranged from 200 to nearly 600 per minute.

Nordenfelt produced three to six barrel machine guns. The mechanism was more or less the same for each variation. The barrels lay side by side and loading and firing was operated by a lever that worked backwards and forwards. The hopper was above the gun. When the lever was

Mitrailleuse mounted with shields at the Siege of Paris, 1871. The multiple barrels show clearly at the muzzle.

2nd Lieutenant V. A. Browning firing a Browning machine gun invented by his father.

SIEGE OF PARIS: MITRAILLEUSE WITH SHIELDS.

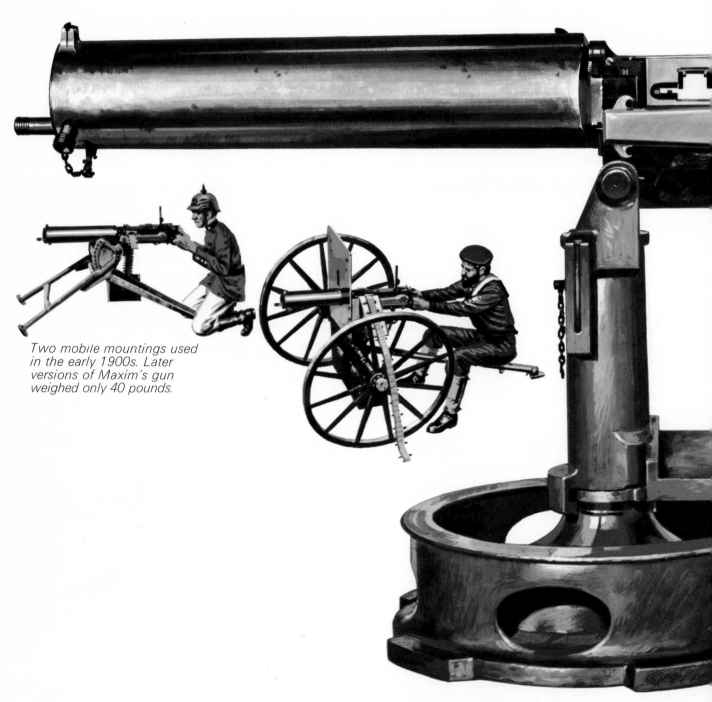

Two mobile mountings used in the early 1900s. Later versions of Maxim's gun weighed only 40 pounds.

pushed forward, a feed from the hopper was brought down and loaded all the barrels simultaneously. The gun was cocked and fired all in the same forward action of the lever. When the lever was pulled back, the spent cartridges were ejected, the bolts withdrawn and the breech made ready for the next feed of live ammunition.

The Nordenfelt became particularly popular with the British navy against the increasing threat of torpedo boats, although it was also used on land. Later, Nordenfelt made several guns with larger calibres and heavier shots.

The first fully automatic machine gun was produced by an American. Hiram S. Maxim patented his design in 1883. For as long as the trigger was pulled the gun would go on firing continuously, with cartridges fed into it from a flexible belt. Loading, firing and ejection of the spent car-

The Maxim machine gun had a rate of fire of up to 650 rounds a minute. Here we show an early model on its heavy, fixed, mounting.

Sir Hiram Maxim proudly displays his original machine gun, patented in 1883.

tridges were all set in motion by the recoil of each shot. On firing, the barrel and recoil frame were driven back about an inch, setting into action the mechanism for reloading the gun.

With a rate of fire up to 650 rounds per minute, the barrel tended to get very hot. Maxim settled this problem by encasing it in a water-cooled jacket. In 1891, a model weighing only 40 pounds was introduced into the British army. This was used in the Boer War, while the Boers them-selves made use of a heavier Maxim machine gun called a 'Pom-pom'. A well-designed war machine could always find a use on either side of any conflict.

The American, gas-operated Lewis gun appeared in 1911 and was used extensively in the First World War. It weighed only 25 pounds and could be handled by one man.

PORTABLE FIREPOWER
The Tommy Gun

Guns have been produced in great diversity and with a wide variety of uses. Although they make use of the same basic principles, each type is a war machine in its own right with a specific task in battle. The siege gun, the anti-tank gun, the anti-aircraft gun, field artillery, the machine gun, the mortar and the infantryman with his rifle – each developed along reciprocal lines of attack and counter-attack, and each development played a new part in new combat situations. So, the infantryman of the 20th Century, armed with new weapons, was a different kind of fighting machine to the arquebusier of the 17th Century.

It was sufficient for the sniper to be armed with a conventional rifle, provided that it was of proven accuracy and range, but it became increasingly desirable for the infantryman to be armed with a lightweight, portable version of the machine gun – a weapon that could produce a high rate of fire, yet be small and compact enough to become the regular equipment of almost every soldier.

The sub-machine gun was developed by the Italians during the First World War and further improved by the Germans, whose MP-18 had a circular magazine with 32 rounds of shot. The explosion of each shot automatically activated the bolt to reject the spent cartridge and insert a new shot.

The renowned Tommy gun was also a sub-machine gun. Its real name was the Thompson machine gun, after the name of its designer, an American general. Equipped with several different magazines, this could fire up to 100 rounds a minute. For convenience, it could also be fitted with a folding butt.

The Tommy gun was first produced in 1920 and was widely used in the Second World War. It was replaced by the M-3 sub-machine gun, with a calibre of ·45 inches and a magazine of 30 rounds. The M-3 had one surprise: there was an extra barrel that could be used with captured German ammunition. Nothing, if at all possible, was ever wasted in time of war.

Guns for Resistance

A different style of war demanded a different machine. For the French Resistance against German occupation there was the sten-gun, light, collapsible and easy to produce. Armed with this, the Maquisards worked undercover to undermine the German hold on their country. The sten

FBI agent firing a Thompson sub-machine gun.

had a magazine with 32 rounds of 9-mm ammunition and could fire at a rate of over 500 rounds per minute, with a killing range of 200 yards. It could be broken down for concealment into four parts: magazine, barrel unit, body and stock.

The sten was not only a resistance weapon. It was used extensively as the standard British sub-machine gun.

A modern type of the sub-machine gun is the Uzi, used by the Israelis in the 1973 Middle East war, and named after its designer, Major Uziel Gal. Short and handy to use, the Uzi has a rate of 650 rounds per minute and made a great reputation for itself during that war.

Even before then, there was a leaning toward a rifle that could double, on automatic fire, as a sub-machine gun. The Soviet AK-47, used by the Arabs, is one of the best of these guns. It is also called the Kalashnikov assault rifle and has a magazine of 30 rounds with a rate of fire of 600 rounds per minute.

On the Israeli side, the Galil has a rate of over 600 rounds per minute and 30- or 50-round magazines. It has an additional device, incorporated into the design – not essential to the machine itself, you might think at first, but encouraging to the efficiency of its handler, and so to the machine as a whole. This is a bottle opener, which the designer added when he noticed soldiers using the lip of their magazine for that purpose.

Bren-gunner in action from the ruins of a house in Douet, Normandy, 1944.

Several types of sten-gun were made, not only for the Resistance. Here are Mark I, II, III and V.

French St Chamond 400-mm rail gun

THE BIG GUNS
Giants of War

The great siege machines of the 15th Century made their reappearance in a more sophisticated and even more destructive form during the end of the 19th Century and particularly during the First World War, as the opposing armies attempted to batter each other into submission. Instead, their massive guns served mainly to tear up into an impassable morass the countryside of France and Belgium. The terrible stark landscapes of First World War Europe characterized that war, and the big guns played an awesome part in the creation of that character.

The German guns dominated the list of the mammoths and, against the Krupp-built monsters, even the French giants were inadequate. Two of the biggest French guns were the St Chamond 400-mm rail gun and the Babignolles 320-mm rail gun. The second had a range of a little under two miles and fired shells between 800 and 1,000 pounds, but the first had a range of nearly 10 miles and fired shells between one-and-a-half and two thousand pounds each.

In between these came the French 370-mm mortar, with a shell of 250 pounds but a range of

five miles. It had the advantage of a quick rate of fire – approximately one round every two minutes. But it required a crew of 16 men to operate it at maximum efficiency. The 370-mm was used effectively by the French at Verdun.

Against the French at the opening of war in 1914, the Germans brought the thunder of their 420-mm howitzers, which appeared on the battlefield as soon as hostilities began. Their shells weighed nearly a ton and they slammed into the defences of Liège with marked results and to the considerable surprise of the French, for the Germans had kept their new weapon a great secret from their enemies.

Special tractors and carriages were made to carry the considerable weight of the gun, which had to be broken down into its component parts before transportation. Rail was often used as an alternative means of transport. The barrel alone weighed over 20 tons, the cradle weighed about 15 tons and the mount for the gun another 20 tons. There was also a base of 12 tons as well as ammunition and ancillary equipment – and the crew. 'Big Bertha', as the gun was sometimes

called, totalled over 70 tons and could fire a round every six or seven minutes.

The Germans had announced that the 420-mm was a naval gun, which accounted for the Allied surprise when they found themselves facing it on dry land. Another supposedly 'naval' gun was the 380-mm long range gun that the Germans used later at Verdun. This had a range of nearly 30 miles and could be used to fire well over the front lines of both armies onto communication and transport links to the rear of the enemy.

The Bombardment of Paris

The greatest First World War gun of all was the extraordinary Paris gun that had a range of 75 miles and was created especially for the bombardment of Paris. The idea was first put forward in the spring of 1916 but the first shell did not fall on Paris until Saturday, March 23, 1918. Between those two dates, the Krupp factories were in a fever of calculations and designs.

In order to achieve the range it was necessary greatly to increase the initial velocity of the shell and make it perform a trajectory that would make use of the thinner atmosphere high above the earth. The barrel consisted of one 15-inch barrel, over 55 feet long, into which was put another barrel, or 'inner tube', with a calibre of 8·26 inches, and which, with a small tube or chase added on to the base of the barrel, extended the overall length of the gun barrel to about 112 feet. In order to keep all this straight, a series of struts along the barrel held it braced.

The gun was aimed at an angle of 50 degrees, in order for the shot to enter the lighter atmosphere at an angle of 45 degrees, the angle of maximum efficiency. Allowance had to be made for the rotation of the earth and it was vital that the shell left the barrel at one mile per second. All these considerations had to be taken into account in preparing the gun.

The shell itself weighed 228 pounds and had a triple cartridge which contained about 500 pounds of powder. Since the elevation of the gun remained unaltered, the amount of powder had to be varied with each shot to lessen or increase the range and to compensate for cold or hot weather as well – and this was very important –

for the wear on the inside of the barrel after every shot. It was estimated that the gun would be useless after about 60–65 shots, for each of which the shell would have to weigh a little more. To solve this problem, each shell was numbered. So precise were the calculations involved and the attention to detail was so perfect that it was possible to tell exactly where the shell landed merely by reading off the pressure gauges attached to the barrel and ascertaining the pressure in the barrel at each shot.

Bombs from a Clear Sky

Three of the Paris guns were set up in great secret, carefully camouflaged, in the forests near Laon, 70 miles from the heart of Paris. Their aim was to demoralize the Parisians while a massive German offensive got under way. At a little after 7.16 on the morning of March 23, the first of the guns fired from behind a thick smoke screen, additionally camouflaged by a stepped-up barrage from nearby artillery. The shell reached an altitude of 12 miles in 25 seconds, travelling at a speed of 3,000 feet per second. It left the barrel at just under the required speed of a mile per second, or 5,280 feet per second. A maximum height of 24 miles was reached in 90 seconds, at which point the shell was travelling at 2,250 feet per second. On its downward curve its speed increased to over 3,000 feet per second again, 12 miles above Paris and its unaware citizens.

The shell struck the paving stones outside No. 6 Quai de Seine in the 19th Arrondissement just before 7.20, after a flight of 92 miles in 176 seconds. The Quai de Seine was 67·6 miles round the curvature of the earth from the forest hideout in Laon. No one was injured and the explosion was barely noticed; to those who did notice, it sounded like a single bomb from a plane too high to be seen, for the sky was clear.

A second shell landed within 15 minutes; further shells followed, spattered around the city, at approximately 15-minute intervals. People were injured and killed. Still assuming that it was an air-raid, though mystified by the lack of sound or sight of aeroplanes, the people of Paris took shelter when the sirens went, about an hour after the first shell.

At 10 o'clock the War Ministry announced that 'a few enemy aircraft, flying at very high altitudes, succeeded in crossing the lines and attacking Paris. They were immediately engaged by our fighter aircraft, both those from the entrenched camp and those from the front.

Bombs are reported to have been dropped at several points and there are some casualties'. If fighter aircraft had gone up to investigate, it was unlikely that they had found anything.

In view of the remarkable novelty of a gun of such extreme range – a range of 23 miles had previously been the longest experienced in the war – the experts were, in fact, commendably quick in tracking down the source of the explosions. By plotting the positions of the explosions and by alerting the sound-ranging units at the front line (they located enemy batteries through highly sensitive listening devices), they knew approximately what they were up against by early afternoon of that first day. By early evening, batteries of 12-inch railway guns were on their way to the nearest available point at the front to counteract the threat.

Over 20 shells fell on Paris each of the first two days of the bombardment, although on the second day, Sunday, a second gun joined in. This gun blew up the next day and killed most of its crew. There was a lull for three days after that, until firing resumed on Good Friday and produced the greatest slaughter so far.

At 4.30 p.m. a shell struck the old Church of Saint-Gervais in the Rue Miron, opposite the Hotel de Ville, where several hundred people were praying. The explosion destroyed a pillar and a great chunk of the vaulting so that a large area of the roof came down on top of the congregation. Nearly 90 people were killed and another 70 more injured.

It is possible that this dramatic hit was achieved by a third gun, for by this time the first gun was worn out. The experts had been right: one gun wore out after 50 shots, another after about 60. In all, after four intermittent bombardments, 367 shells were fired on Paris and landed on or nearby the city, being directly responsible for about 250 deaths and a further 620 wounded. But these figures barely reflect the corrosive effect that this long range barrage must have had on the morale of those Parisians who experienced the terror of being struck in the heart of their city from behind an enemy line supposed to be a safe 70 miles away.

The last shell fell on August 9, 1918. But the advancing Allied troops found no significant trace of the guns, which had been demolished as carefully as they had been assembled months before in preparation for the bombardment.

Germany followed up its First World War successes with a 280-mm gun with a range of

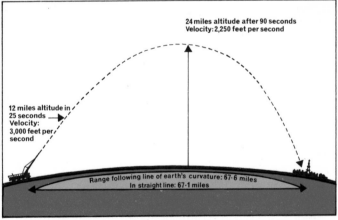

24 miles altitude after 90 seconds
Velocity: 2,250 feet per second

12 miles altitude in
25 seconds
Velocity:
3,000 feet per
second

Range following line of earth's curvature: 67·6 miles
In straight line: 67·1 miles

nearly 40 miles and a giant 800-mm cannon 'Dora' with a shell 25-feet-long, a range of nearly 30 miles and a crew of about 250 men. America developed the Long Tom. But the shells from these guns did not have the psychological impact of those first bombardments in March 1918. Even less did they cause the consternation of complete novelty that had characterized the use of Mahomet's great siege cannon outside Constantinople, 460 years before.

Top: German 420-mm siege gun, nicknamed Big Bertha, of the type used against Liège.
Above left: Artist's impression of the German Paris Gun, with a range of over 70 miles.
Above right: Diagram showing the trajectory and range of shells fired by the Paris Gun.

ARMOURED FIGHTING VEHICLES
The Balance of Efficiency

Since mobile war machines of any kind had been first devised, military thinkers and engineers had been trying to strike a happy balance between the amount of firepower that could be exerted by a particular machine, the amount of protection it had from the firepower of another machine, and its mobility.

This balance was rarely achieved. Early cavalry were lightly armed and highly mobile, but unprotected; early siege machines were well-protected, sometimes well-armed, but virtually immobile; elephants had some protection, could be heavily armed with spearmen and bowmen, and were mobile but erratic. For a hundred years or so the medieval knight seemed to provide the ideal answer until, in response to the penetrative power of the arrow, his body armour became absurdly heavy and, with the introduction of firearms, totally useless. He was compelled to disencumber himself of his overweight equipment.

His means of mobility – the horse – was always vulnerable. Early concepts for well-protected, horse-powered machines were imaginative but generally impractical. Among the most ingenious inventors was Leonardo da Vinci, who made several drawings for armoured fighting vehicles. What was needed toward the end of the 19th Century was a machine driven by mechanical power strong enough to carry sufficient armour to stop a bullet from a rifle or machine gun, while

Rolls Royce cars were quickly turned to wartime use. A Rolls Royce light armoured car at Abbéville, in 1916.

at the same time able to move at reasonable speeds and pack its own effective punch.

From Steam Carriage to Traction Wheel

The invention of the steam engine opened possibilities toward the design of such a machine. The first person to realize the potential of steam as mechanical power for military purposes was James Cugnot, who put his steam carriage at the disposal of the French army in 1770. Because of the machine's unreliability, Cugnot was not taken up on his offer.

Meanwhile ideas for traction wheels were developed, though largely on paper only. The theory of the traction wheel was that a wheel should be surrounded by a linked series of small tracks that would, as they revolved with the wheel, serve as a self-contained roadway along which the vehicle could travel, regardless of the rough surface of the ground.

George Kale recorded a double-wheeled concept in 1825 and a man called Gomper planned a single tracked wheel six years later. Two other single tracked wheels were designed, by Dunlop in 1861 and by Clark, almost 30 years later. They were strange looking contraptions that never went into production.

One or two steam tractors made their appearance at the end of the 19th Century but it was the introduction of the petrol engine that gave a real

An armoured steam-roller from the 1870s.

boost to the armoured fighting vehicle. It was a motley collection of machines that appeared between 1890 and the development of the first real tank during the First World War but some of them are worth a closer look.

The Motor War Car

One of the first was Fowler's armoured road loco-motive, with a train of armour-plated waggons (inspired by armoured railway trains) used during the Boer War of 1899–1902.

In 1902, F. R. Simms, an Englishman, produced his Motor War Car – a grand-sounding name for an odd-looking machine, shaped like an upturned boat hull, with two Maxim machine guns at one end and a large Maxim 'pom-pom' at the other. A crew of four was normal but, if required, the guns could be taken out and the vehicle used as a troop carrier for 12 men.

The Motor War Car was first demonstrated at a Press Conference at the Crystal Palace, London, where its capabilities were acknowledged as being impressive, although the War Office showed no further interest. The die for a new military button or a 'dustman's cap' for the Guards,

claimed one journal of the day, were of much more interest to the officers of the War Office than Simms' Motor War Car.

This was not Simm's first armoured vehicle, however. In 1899, he had produced the de Dion-Bouton powered quadri-cycle, with a Maxim machine gun. In fact, credit for the Motor War Car did not properly belong to Simms – its layout followed drawings produced six years earlier by E. J. Pennington.

Another strange machine that did not get beyond the preliminary stages of a military career was the Armoured Ivel Tractor. This three-wheeled tractor had been the first success-ful, petrol-operated tractor on the market. It was designed by Dan Albone of Biggleswade, Bedford-shire, in 1903; the armoured version appeared three years later. In this version the whole contraption was completely enclosed but, since no weapons seem to have been attached to it, it was probably intended – had it ever been put to use – for towing purposes only. Perhaps it was as well that it was not used: three-wheeled and light in front, it had a nasty tendency to overturn if the load was too heavy.

Top left: A Killen Strait tractor
precariously poised to rise over an
obstacle.
Left: A Davidson Cadillac of 1916.
Above: Lanchester Armoured Car,
of the Royal Naval Air Service,
with machine gun.
Top right: Russian Garfords,
heavily armoured and bristling
with armament, look more like
a column of mechanical science
fiction monsters.
Right: Another famous name
transformed into a military
machine—a 1915 Lancia.

Many of the early armoured cars and fighting vehicles appeared with the names of the great car designers and manufacturers. This was because most armoured vehicles were converted civilian cars, or used the same engines. One example is the Daimler Panzerwagen of 1904, mounted with Maxim machine guns and capable of nearly 30 miles an hour. The Armoured Rolls Royce of 1914 is another example, though the armour on this was only light and it was mounted with one light machine gun. Better armoured Rolls Royces followed the first experiments and Wolseleys joined the ranks.

In France, converted Renaults were commissioned as the First World War opened. American Packards appeared. Fiats, Lanchesters, Lancias and even Cadillacs followed. Some were only lightly armed; others were virtually unrecognizable. Every country brought whatever machines it had to hand and improvised what it did not have.

It was the energy of Winston Churchill that encouraged armoured car production in England during the war. He demanded armoured vehicles to support the Royal Naval Air Service aircraft force in France. The Seabrook armoured lorry, mounted with a three-pounder Vickers semi-automatic gun, was one of the heavier armaments of the period. Despite the weight of the vehicle, the gun was successful in this capacity and Sir John French, Commander of the British Expeditionary Force, requested that more should be sent to France.

The Russian Garford Armoured Car was a massive vehicle, built in Petrograd in 1915 on an imported American Garford chassis. The Garford mounted a 75-mm gun as well as three Maxim machine guns, one beside the 75-mm in the rear turret, the other two behind and to the side of the cab. The whole machine weighed about 11 tons – and probably became bogged down very quickly in bad conditions.

The bigger the vehicle and the more powerful it became, the more likely it was to get stuck in the mud of Russia or Flanders. Barbed wire, trenches, obstacles of every kind, and always the mud – they did not suit these basically conventional wheeled machines, however outrageously redesigned. The answer lay in earlier experiments: a machine with tracks.

THE TANK TAKES TO THE FIELD
Little Willie

The idea of the tank, with all-round tracks to provide the vital need for a vehicle that could traverse small trenches, crush barbed-wire-type defences, withstand machine gun fire and exert its own firepower was put forward by Levavasseur of the French Artillery in 1903 and by Donahue of the Army Service Corps in 1908. In both cases they conceived of an armoured, self-propelled, tracked field gun. In 1911, Burstyn of the Austrian Army and in 1912, de Mole, an Australian, also put forward the idea of a tracked armoured vehicle. In 1914 Lieutenant-Colonel Swinton, a British Engineer, furthered the idea.

The first tracked vehicle was made up of the body of a Delaunay-Belleville armoured car on the chassis of a Killen Strait tractor. This was in Britain, in 1915.

A rhomboidal shape was first suggested by Lieutenant W. G. Wilson of the Royal Naval Air Service, who had been ordered, together with William Tritton of William Foster and Company, of Lincoln, to design an appropriate vehicle to help the Allied push forward in Europe.

Wilson and Tritton's first machine did not, in fact, use a rhomboidal shape. The Tritton Machine, or Little Willie, as it became known, had a rectangular hull set on tracks that were fractionally shorter than the body, with a turret on top. It was powered by a 105 horsepower Daimler six-cylinder engine and was the first

vehicle to be exclusively designed and built as a landship.

The word 'tank' was purposively deceptive, since it was important to maintain the utmost secrecy and to hide the existence of the new machine from the enemy. It was therefore referred to as a 'large water tank for Russia', from which the name 'tank' naturally evolved.

Mother is Rhomboidal

When Little Willie failed to come up to the War Office requirements for obstacle crossing, Wilson began working on his new rhomboidal design, or lozenge shape, with tracks that ran round the top of the hull. This model carried two naval six-pounders as armament, set in turrets at the side of the body; it was powered by a unit similar to that in Little Willie.

Big Willie, or Mother, as it was called – it was also called Wilson's Machine and H.M. Landship Centipede – had its first trials on January 16, 1916 and easily met War Office requirements to cross a ditch eight feet wide and mount a parapet four and a half feet high.

Tanks at Cambrai

Although Field Marshal Sir Douglas Haig ordered the use of tanks in an attack on the Somme in September, 1916, they were not then reliable enough to have anything more than a

Below: French Renault FT17 light tank. These illustrations are not to scale.

Above: German A7V, Sturmpanzerwagen, of 1918, less efficient than Allied tanks.

psychological effect. Individual actions by tanks took the enemy completely by surprise in the first stages of their use, until the Germans grew accustomed to the preparatory stages of a tank attack. Neither individual nor group applications seemed to promise a resounding breakthrough until the tanks were first used in a major role on November 20, 1917, at Cambrai.

In this action, the tanks appeared unheralded by the usual preliminary artillery barrage. Tactics were conceived by Colonel J. F. C. Fuller, the 'Unconventional Soldier', who had a reputation as a military thinker. 474 Mark IV tanks advanced along a broad front about 10 miles wide; they managed to break through the German lines and to penetrate four miles beyond within a few hours. Since an advance of a few hundred *yards* had previously been considered very successful, it is not difficult to imagine the jubilation at such sudden progress. Moreover, infantry losses on the British side were considerably lower than was usual in an attack of this degree, and well below half those of the Germans, who also lost a considerable amount of artillery.

Developed almost simultaneously with the first British invention was the French Schneider, which mounted a 75-mm gun as well as two Hotchkiss machine guns. The first production order was placed in February, 1916, though the tanks did not go into action until April, 1917. It

had a speed of over three-and-a-half miles an hour, weighed over 13½ tons and had a range of 30 miles. One of its characteristics was a metal bar that projected at the front for the purpose of crushing barbed wire. The St Chamond was another successful French tank; it weighed a further 10 tons more than the Schneider. Much lighter than both these was the Renault Mosquito.

The German A7V was equivalent in weight to the St Chamond but not so effective. The Germans suffered badly from a lack of armour throughout the last years of the war.

The Panzer Tanks

By 1939, however, having learnt their lesson, the Germans were far better equipped and their tanks formed the nucleus of the combined mobile striking force, the Panzer division. One German tank was the 'light-medium' Pzkw (*Panzerkampfwagen*) Mark III, with a 37-mm or 50-mm long-barrelled Kwk (*Kampfwagenkanon*).

The Pzkw IV was armed with a 75-mm gun but had armour no stronger than the Mark III. Light armour, in comparison to that of the Allies' tanks, was usually a feature of the German machines. Until they invaded Russia, the Germans thought their tanks were invincible. But the Soviet T-34 stopped them, literally, in their tracks. They had no foreknowledge of the Soviet development, which was simple to produce and to operate and so could be turned out in large numbers and be manned by fairly raw crews. The T-34 had wide tracks for good cross-country performance, a range of 250 miles on the road, armour that was sloped to repel enemy fire, and a 76·2-mm gun.

The Panther was the German answer to the T-34, and the most successful German tank of the war (about 5,000 were produced). But the most famous German tank was probably the Tiger, which for once was well-protected as well as well-armed. This also was designed for the Russian front, although it was used effectively in the West and in North Africa. Weighing 55 tons, it had a speed of 25 miles an hour and mounted a powerful 88-mm gun.

The Tanks of the Allies

On the side of the Allies, the Char B was probably the toughest French tank. It had nearly double the armour of the equivalent German tank and mounted a 75-mm gun. But it had a small turret in which the single operator was overworked. It was also slow.

The British Valentine was used in the desert war but was not fast enough for the German tanks nor heavily enough armed. The Churchill Mark I also suffered from light armament, although its firepower was increased during the war. The chassis of the Churchill was used for a great many special purpose vehicles, as can be seen in the next chapter. Another British tank used in the desert was the Crusader. The Centurion arrived only at the end of the war.

The greatest American contribution in the heavy tank range was the 75-mm Sherman, mechanically reliable and toughly armoured, with a speed just over 20 miles an hour. The Japanese concentrated on light, fast, and small tanks suitable for Pacific warfare on small islands, where foreign tanks found the going almost impossible. The Type-61 medium tank was one of their most useful designs.

Since the war the British Chieftain established a good reputation. One of the standard American medium tanks has been the M-60. The German Leopard, supplied to several armies, is similar in design to the French AMX-30, although more powerful. One of the most modern designs is the Swedish S-tank, with a low profile, hydro-pneumatic suspension and a 105-mm gun – far removed from some of the drawings made by Leonardo da Vinci in anticipation of the first armoured fighting vehicles.

Above: A war-worn German Panther, Model A. Below: Column of Crusader tanks in Western Desert.

Above: The highly effective Russian T-34-85 medium tank.

Right: Sherman Crab II, fitted with flail as a mine-destroying device. There were various adaptations of this system.

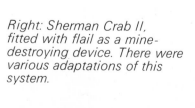

Above: 88mm gun mounted on Tiger P. chassis.
Below: British Matilda tank.

Above: 'Carpet Roller' attached to tank chassis.

SPECIAL DUTY TANKS
The Trench Annihilator

The tank proved its usefulness as a machine in assault over rough terrain against armed resistance; the revolving turret, mounted with varying sizes of guns and placed on a tracked chassis, became, by the Second World War, one of the most important assets of every army. But the concept of a tracked vehicle could be adapted in many ways to other duties and a variety of machines appeared during the war that took the tank a long way from what was originally conceived in the name the Germans gave to it during the First World War: *Schutzengrabenvernichtungspanzerkraftwagen*, or 'protected trench annihilation armoured vehicle'.

Nearest in purpose to the tank was the Self Propelled Gun, or SPG. This was simpler in design than the tank and had no turret mechanism It mounted a heavy gun but had no secondary armament. Its purpose was to act as fast moving artillery support for infantry.

After their confrontation with the Soviet T-34s, the Germans stepped up their production of SPGs, which began to take precedence over ordinary tank production. SPGs became increasingly powerful but less manoeuvrable.

One of the heaviest of the German SPGs was an adaptation of the Tiger, sometimes called an Elephant. It was a powerful tank-hunter itself, built in 1943 on a Porsche Tiger chassis and mounting an 88-mm gun. Another adaptation was that of the French Char B chassis, which the Germans mounted with a 105-mm gun. On their side, the Soviets mounted a 122-mm gun on their SU-122, which used their T-34 chassis, and a 152-mm gun on their JSU-152.

The Mine-destroyers

Encased in metal, tanks were highly vulnerable to mines. Many adaptations of the tank applied to mine-clearance. A minefield was as much of an obstacle as a trench system or a surface barrier, and pathways for the infantry had to be made before an advance could begin.

One of the strangest-looking of these machines was the British Scorpion, which was built on the chassis of the Matilda tank. Stretching out before it, two long arms supported a revolving drum on which were fitted several sets of chain flails that beat the ground in front of the tank. The flailing chains hopefully made contact with the mines

Over: Pzkw IVs pass Bren gun-carrier in the desert

and exploded them at a safe distance from the vehicle.

The Crab was another landmine sweeper. This was based on the Sherman chassis and could clear a pathway about 10 feet wide with a set of chains similar to the Scorpion attached to a drum and held in front of the tank. But an alternative attachment to the Matilda was the mine-roller, which consisted of sets of rollers pushed forward in front of the tank on long arms. The advantage of these over the flails was that they more precisely simulated the *weight* of the tank – and it was weight, more than contact, that was essential in order to detonate the mines.

Carpets and Crocodiles

To help wheeled vehicles over soft patches of ground, and particularly sand, there was the Bobbin, an attachment to the Churchill chassis that was capable of laying a carpet over the ground. The carpet was almost 10 feet wide and made of canvas.

Another obstacle clearer, and another adaptation of the Churchill chassis – the Churchill was the ideal tank for these adaptations – was the bridge-layer. The SBG bridge, carried in front

of the chassis and held up by a wire to the back of the chassis, could be laid over a gap 30 feet wide in about 30 seconds; it could also support up to 40 tons when laid against a parapet 15 feet high. The Valentine was another bridge-layer.

Yet another Churchill adaptation, the Churchill Crocodile, mounted a lethal flame thrower with a range of 120 yards. Fuel was carried in a special trailer towed behind and pumped through to the gun. When the fuel was used up, the trailer could be jettisoned and the tank's gun used as normal.

Towing of a different kind was the special duty of the Churchill ARV, or Armoured Recovery Vehicle; the Sherman was similarly equipped with towing gear and tools for the recovery of valuable tanks from the battlefield. Breakdowns could as easily occur as battle scars: the ARVs were kept busy all the time.

Remote Control

In a more offensive capacity, the remote controlled tank was developed during the Second World War. It had a similar function and effect, you might suppose, as the fire-ship of the early days of sail, or the kamikaze plane of the

Above: One of the many Churchill adaptations was the Crocodile flame thrower.

Right: Tanks made useful mobile platforms for rocket launchers. Shermans are being used here.

Left: Back view of a Sherman Duplex Drive with screens half way up.

Japanese. It was the Japanese who tried out one model before the war – the Nagayama. But during the war it was the Germans who laid greatest emphasis on this type of machine. Remote controlled tanks had small chassis, without turrets, and were filled with high explosive. They were used best against enemy fortifications, although they could also be used against tanks themselves. One German model was the Goliath; a later model was the NSU Springer.

The B-IV was also radio-controlled, although it could, if required, be driven by one man. In this case no suicidal tactics were necessary. The machine held a block in front of it, filled with explosive. The block could be detached and left against a fortification or barricade while the tank made a judicious retreat and watched the explosion from a safe distance.

The Amphibious Machine

Most important for beach landings and river crossings were amphibious tanks. One of the oddest convertible devices, contrived for the D-Day offensive, was the Duplex Drive, that could be fitted to the Sherman tank. When fitted, it gave the tank the shape of something between a perambulator and a playpen. But the collapsible canvas screen – the parallel with the pram grows stronger – kept the water out and buoyed up the tank, which had the additional drive of two propellers and could 'sail' at over four knots.

The Japanese in particular required to adapt their tanks to the amphibious warfare of the Pacific. One Japanese machine was fitted with wooden floats shaped to a bow. Once on land the floats could be blown out of the way.

The Soviet Union also paid considerable attention to amphibious warfare as, more recently, have the Swedes. The Soviet T-37 was fitted with balsa wood floats; the modern PT-76 has a boat-shaped hull and is powered by hydra-jets. Other amphibious armed vehicles are often conversions from armoured cars, with boat hulls and wheels. The American Commando is one of these.

Some tanks are now equipped with rockets. A conversion of the French AMX-13 used rockets mounted forward as well as its usual armament of guns. The rockets were guided on to the target by means of a thin 'fishing line', which unwound as the missile shot toward its target. Other machines use radio-controlled rockets and are essentially rocket-launchers only.

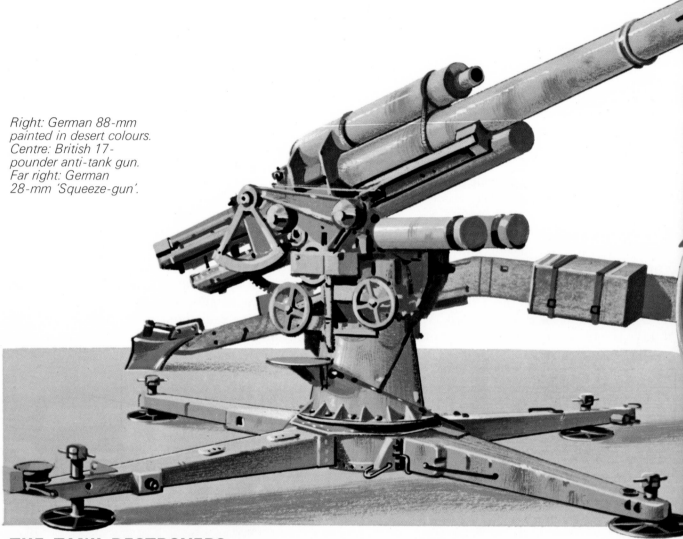

Right: German 88-mm painted in desert colours. Centre: British 17-pounder anti-tank gun. Far right: German 28-mm 'Squeeze-gun'.

THE TANK DESTROYERS
Adapted for Destruction

By now it has become evident that one machine requires a reciprocal machine to counteract it. The tank presented formidable defensive armour for any conventional gun to penetrate. Machine guns and rifle fire were inadequate – the tank, after all, had been especially designed to render them inadequate. So it became necessary to create a new type of gun with a shell that could smash tank armour.

The British army began the Second World War with a 2-pounder gun, which was then replaced by a 6-pounder and finally a 17-pounder; the Germans had a variety of successful anti-tank guns, among which was an adaptation of their highly efficient anti-aircraft 88-mm. The British

17-pounder was bulky, a severe handicap for a gun that it was vital to conceal while lying in wait for its target, but it could knock out a German Tiger tank at a range of 1,000 yards and it had a maximum range of about 3,000 yards. It was probably the most useful of the Allies' anti-tank guns and was mounted, at a later stage, on a variety of tanks, including the Sherman Firefly.

The German 88-mm was one of the most lethal and feared guns in the war. Rommel used it to great effect in his campaign in the desert, in particular when he found himself over-reached and under heavy attack by the Allies. As well as being used as a stationary piece of artillery against tanks, it was also fitted to the Tiger I and

II and could penetrate three inches of armour at 1,000 yards. No Allied tank could withstand the 88-mm, which acquired a reputation amounting almost to a myth among those against whom it was used.

Armour-piercing Shells

The most important part of any anti-tank gun is clearly its shell; if guns and armour were not to vie continually in ever-increasing weight until both became unmanageable, then shells had to be made that, without increasing in size, could penetrate armour of almost any thickness.

Armour-piercing shot was commonly used in 1939 – solid shot that broke through the armour

of a tank by sheer force. The stronger the armour, the greater the force with which the shot needed to be fired: the stalemate situation. Armour-piercing shells, on the other hand, also penetrated by force but subsequently blew up inside the tank to cause considerably more damage.

Squeeze Guns and Sabots

Aids to penetration included a soft-capped shell that spread the impact over a wider surface of the target. Another advance was a tungsten carbide tipped shell – harder than steel – fired from a tapered barrel. The Germans used this technique in their 28-mm Panzerbusche 41, or 'Squeeze gun'. The tungsten core was contained in a light alloy casing that was squeezed, as it was fired through the barrel of the gun, from a calibre of 28-mm at the breech to 21-mm at the muzzle. This squeezing increased the velocity of the shot with a subsequent increase in its capacity to penetrate armour.

Another strange shot was the AP (armour-piercing) Discarding Sabot, used by the 6-pounder and 17-pounder. The light alloy sabot, or outer case of the shot, broke away from the steel shot itself as soon as it left the barrel, leaving the shot to continue at increased velocity toward the target. The large outer core helped the shot to attain a high velocity within the barrel, while the small core could more easily maintain that velocity in flight.

The hollow-charge shell, an even more effective anti-tank projectile, was one which the Germans in particular adopted with enthusiasm. In the 18th Century, a Norwegian engineer had discovered that when he slightly hollowed out the face of an explosive charge it would cut deeper than usual into a rockface. He used this technique for blasting purposes. In 1880, an American, called Monroe, discovered that a similar phenomenon could be achieved against armour plate. He called this the 'Monroe Effect', but it wasn't until some Swiss gave a demonstration of the impact of the Monroe Effect against tank armour, in 1938, that its full military significance became apparent.

The hollow-charge shell consists of a hemispherical forward surface lined with a thin piece of metal and protected by a nose cone. On impact, the cone detonates the explosive charge behind the projectile, which is concentrated by the effect of the hemisphere into a jet of explosive gas and metal that accelerates to tremendous velocity within the hollow space between hemisphere and nose cone. It is this concentrated velocity that gives the shell its penetrative capability. In that it gains this velocity from the nature of the shell rather than, necessarily, the power of the gun that fires it, the hollow-charge shell can be used in a variety of weapons – as, for instance, the 68 Grenade, which could be fired from an infantry rifle and was in production at the beginning of the war to great advantage.

The 'Bazooka'

The recoilless gun was widely used in heavy artillery as well as in order to provide the infantry with their own anti-tank machine. An infantry soldier, easily manoeuvrable, easy to hide, was the ideal launching pad for the covert attack on a tank. Until the recoilless gun appeared, most anti-tank weapons had been far too heavy to carry. Of necessity, they carried with them – in the gun carriage – the full paraphenalia of springs and shock absorbers required by the need to cope with the recoil of the gun.

The principle of the recoilless gun had been realized during the First World War by Commander Davis of the U.S. Navy. His invention was used by the British in aircraft against Zeppelins, an area of combat to which it was particularly well suited because of its lightness.

The recoil was avoided in a primitive but effective way. The gun had two barrels, one pointing in either direction. As the shot was fired forward from one barrel, a similar weight of buckshot and grease was fired backward from the other barrel. The two shots cancelled out each other's recoil. By increasing the speed of the reaction shot, its weight could be lessened until it became merely a fast stream of gas, which would still balance the recoil from the forward shot.

The American 2·36-inch recoilless rocket-launcher, or 'bazooka', was one weapon that provided the advantages of the recoilless gun for the infantryman and gave him the ability to

Below: U.S. TOW missile uses recoilless launcher and is guided by two nearly invisible wires.

knock out a tank. It fired a hollow-charge projectile with great effect almost 400 yards. The Germans later adopted an 88-mm recoilless rocket-launcher, the Panzerschreck, that fired a projectile of seven pounds, about twice the weight of the bazooka.

In the 1973 Arab-Israeli war, hollow-charge shells were still being used and will, no doubt, be used again. Recoilless weapons were also in use in that conflict. One of the more effective of these was the Israeli 105-mm anti-tank rifle, which was mounted on a jeep.

Above: Recoilless rocket launchers mounted on trucks in action in forest land.

AIMED AT THE SKY
The Threat from the Air

The growth of airpower during the First World War and the rapid acceleration of that growth between the wars was a great deal more menacing than the development of the tank. The guns turned on the sky above them and adapted themselves once more to a whole range of specialized needs in order to face the new threat.

The anti-aircraft guns of the First World War were largely of one type; they had an approximately equal ceiling and an approximately equal rate of fire. The aircraft against which they were matched were only of limited capability. The British 13-pounder had an elevation of 80 degrees; that is, it could be aimed up to 10 degrees off the vertical (the potential 'elevation' of a gun is always the angle between the horizontal and its maximum elevation). The German 77-mm, that fired a 15-pound shell, had an elevation of only 70 degrees, as did the French 75-mm and the powerful German 88-mm of the First World War, although the British 3-inch had an elevation of 90 degrees. All could be traversed around a full 360 degrees.

The 13-pounder fired 6–10 rounds per minute, at a muzzle velocity (the speed at which the shell left the muzzle of the gun) of 1,700 feet per second, with a vertical range of 13,000 feet. This might be compared with the 3-inch, that fired 15 rounds per minute at a muzzle velocity of 2,500 feet per second, with a vertical range of 18,000 feet.

These figures point to the specialized needs of the anti-aircraft, or AA gun: a high ceiling, or vertical range; a high rate of fire to throw around a fast moving attacker; a relatively high muzzle velocity in order that the projectile should arrive at its target in the shortest possible time, thus lessening the chance of error in aiming ahead of the target; and the maximum possible elevation. (Naturally, this last made loading difficult, if the gun was not to be brought down to a lower elevation between each shot.)

Light and Heavy Fire

During the Second World War, two types of AA gun were developed; lighter guns to counteract fast, low-flying aircraft; heavier guns to reach up to the high-flying bombers. The successful German heavy 88-mm reverted, as we have already seen, to use as an anti-tank gun, with equal, if not greater, success. But the equivalent British 3·7-inch AA gun remained in use almost exclusively as an anti-aircraft weapon; its poten-

British 13-pounder in action during First World War

tial effect against German tanks was never realized. Another heavy gun was the German 105-mm, with a rate of fire of three rounds per minute and a ceiling of about 40,000 feet, slightly less than the 88-mm. The largest American AA gun during that war was the 120-mm, which could, if necessary, be fired by remote control.

In contrast to these, the Germans had a light 37-mm Flak gun, with a rate of 150 rounds per minute, and the Allies had a 40-mm Bofors with a rate of 120 rounds per minute and an effective altitude of 12,000 feet. Flak, incidentally, is an abbreviation for German 'anti-aircraft gun', or *Fliegerabwehrkanone*. The Bofors could also be used to fire tracer bullets. The 20-mm Oerlikon cannon, with a rate of 650 rounds per minute, was used by the Allies on tanks and ships in every field of the war and was also adopted by the Americans. The Germans had an equivalent 20-mm AA gun with a higher rate of fire. The 20-mm Flakvierling (quadruple gun) had a rate of over 700 rounds per minute.

Although anti-aircraft guns are still used against low-flying, fast planes (during the 1973 Arab-Israeli war, the Arabs made use of the successful Soviet twin 57-mm, with a rate of 120 rounds per minute per barrel), the missile has largely taken over the duties of air defence.

The SAM Missile

The SAM missile is probably one of the best known and most effective of this new type of war machine. Variations of this guided missile were used by the Arabs against Israeli air attacks and had ranges between 15 and 25 miles. They would appear to be the complete answer to air attack: planes can be brought down before they reach their target. But new developments in attack will inevitably follow, and the SAM missile will have to adapt to a new counter-machine.

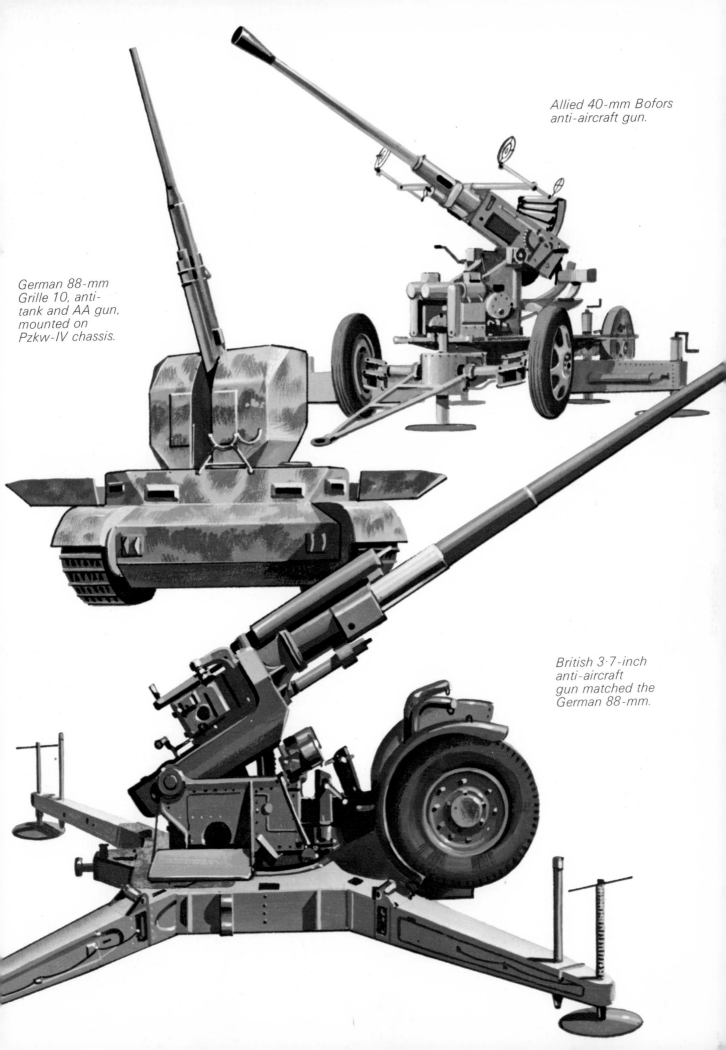

Allied 40-mm Bofors
anti-aircraft gun.

German 88-mm
Grille 10, anti-
tank and AA gun,
mounted on
Pzkw-IV chassis.

British 3·7-inch
anti-aircraft
gun matched the
German 88-mm.

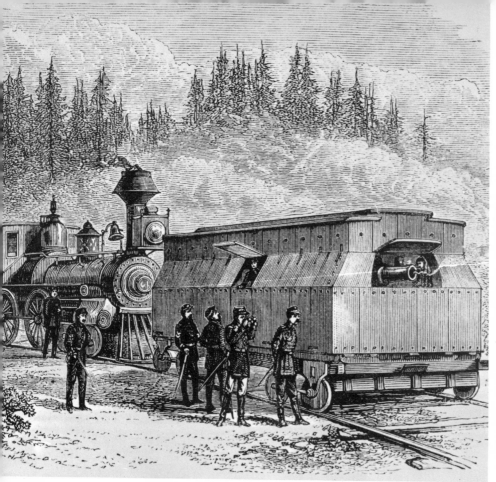

WAR ON RAILS
Piling up at the Front

The steam railway was not invented for military use but its military possibilities were very soon realized and it made possible the rapid transportation of huge numbers of troops and massive equipment. During the 1840s, railway communication links were busily constructed in almost every country that could afford to do so. Once the track was laid, there was at last at their disposal a method of transport that would not become bogged down in the mud, however heavy its load.

Construction programmes were largely intended for civilian passengers and trade, but at the back of every government's mind was the consideration that the railway would also be used in time of war. It was the Prussians who immediately seized on the implications of the new machine and first put it to general military use, when, in 1846, they moved 12,000 men, with horses and guns, to Cracow. Two years later, when the European revolutions of 1848 broke out, Austria, France and Russia also turned with varying degrees of enthusiasm to the railways.

By making possible large troop movements quickly to the front line, the railways were also directly responsible for the increased slaughter that ensued. Tactical manoeuvring was made difficult not only by the sheer number of troops

Left: Federal railway battery from the American Civil War: a war machine with a new impact.
Centre: British troops arriving at Victoria Station, London, on leave during the 1914–18 War.
Right: Heavily armoured train. Armour and armament make it look more like a tank on rails.

arriving but by the inevitable accumulation of soldiers at set points at the end of established lines of transportation. The troops piled up at predetermined destinations from which they were rushed into battle, often without further deployment.

Troop movements of this nature were made at the bloody battle of Solferino, in 1859, during the Franco-Austrian war. In a headlong, almost suicidal, clash between the two armies, there were altogether about 40,000 casualties – almost a quarter of the total number of troops in the field – an appalling proportion.

Similar slaughter occurred during the American Civil War – the machine guns and artillery combined to add to the slaughter – and, in part at least was caused by similar massed troop

movements to limited disembarkation points. The important part to be played by the railways in future wars was shown from the start. At Bull Run, the arrival of Confederate reserves by rail at a crucial moment of setback turned the tide of the battle against the Federals and produced a rout that continued all the way to Washington. But the Confederates failed subsequently to utilize their railway system to the full, a failure that significantly affected their ultimate defeat.

Again, during the Prussian war with France, in 1870, Prussian victories were made possible by extensive use of railways, which enabled great numbers of soldiers to be brought to the Front at short notice. Since France failed to use such a comprehensive rail system, Prussia's advantage was unchallenged. The First World War saw similar massed troop movements by rail, once again increasing the slaughter to gigantic proportions, as both sides put into use the systems they had been preparing ostensibly for civilian use in the preceding years.

The Railway Guns

The Germans, with a wide railway gauge able to take heavy loads, also put the railways to use to transport their giant artillery. Some of these guns were permanently fixed to a bed set on railway wheels. Others were brought to the Front by rail. The lethal 420-mm and the Paris Gun both used rail transport, though the first could as well be transported by road. The French St Chamond and Batignolle also used a rail bed, as did the German giants of the Second World War, being too heavy for anything else.

Russia laid down extensive railway links to cover the vast distances necessary for communications over her enormous territories. One problem of an invading army was whether or not the same gauge or width of rail was used by both countries. The Russians used a narrower gauge than the Germans, partly on purpose to stop German stock using Russian railways in case of invasion.

Inevitably, as railways became increasingly important for troops, guns, food and equipment, they also became major targets for enemy attack. To blow up a railway link was the aim of every guerilla movement, since to do so was to cut off the lifeblood of an army. To appropriate and make use of the enemy's own system was equally the aim of every attacking force. The railways were fought over as prized possessions, a machine of great value to whomever controlled it.

THE GREAT DEFENCE LINES
Stalemate at the Front

The great entrenched lines of the First and Second World War, with their concrete and barbed wire barricades, slit trenches and pill-box fortifications, from which the defence stared out at similar lines across an artillery-torn no-man's wasteland caused, or were intended to cause, the great stalemates of those wars. Compared to such defence lines, Wellington's Lines of Torres Vedras and Vauban's series of star-shaped forts seemed unambitious projects.

These entrenchments were virtually immovable. They were well-armed, they were covered by artillery from behind, they were strongly defended or bravely contested; they were unwieldy creations but they were intended as machines of defence, not attack.

The Hindenburg Line

The Hindenburg Line, which was organized by the Germans during the winter of 1916/1917 did to some extent attempt to remain elastic. It stretched 60 miles from Arras to Vailly on the River Aisne, confronting the major areas of Allied attack. In an allocated battle zone, forward artillery posts, garrisons, infantry, barbed wire and artillery support all played their part but were intended always to give and take where necessary, to retreat and counter-attack, to hold where the line could.

The Hindenburg Line was unfinished when the Allies started their major offensive in the spring of 1917, but it held off many assaults and tied the Allies down to a wearying and highly destructive campaign of trench warfare and artillery-pitted mud. This was the time of the greatest slaughter, when in one battle alone, against these sponge-like entrenchments, which absorbed the dead and their blood so greedily, there were well over half a million British, German and French casualties.

The tank offensive at Cambrai in November 1917 proved that the Hindenburg Line was not invincible but several more major battles were necessary, together with immense loss of life, before the line was finally broken completely and the Germans worn out to defeat.

The Maginot Line is Bypassed

Learning their lessons from the First World War, the opposing forces prepared for the Second by even greater lines of defence, each hoping that the enemy would exhaust themselves in futile attack. The French Maginot Line, which took about 10 years to complete, stretched almost 200 miles. It was only a narrow barrier but it was equipped with forts, some of them underground, artillery, barbed wire and machine guns. Facing it, the weaker and never completed Siegfried Line, or West Wall, continued to make use of the German philosophy of flexibility.

Above left: British troops enter a fort on the Maginot Line in November 1939.
Above right: American combat troops inspect a battle-scarred fortress on the Maginot Line.
Left: American soldiers swing a four-gun battery of the Maginot Line eastward against the Nazis a few hours after capturing them from the Germans.
Right: U.S. Reconnaissance troops wait behind captured enemy pillbox in the Maginot Line.

When the German Panzer divisions swept round the end of the Maginot Line, through Belgium, in the lightning campaign of May and June, 1940, the ineffectiveness of the Line was revealed. The Allies were driven back to the sea and across the Channel, where they regathered their strength behind the natural and far more effective barrier of the Channel itself. Once France was occupied by the Germans, the Maginot Line became little more than a mockery.

The age of static defence lines was made redundant by the increased mobility of armoured divisions and the increased importance of air-power. Although the actual solidity of the line could not be questioned, since evidence of it is still visible today, it remained no longer a valid war machine.

THE THRUST OF THE PANZERS
The Tank as Spearhead

The German panzer, or armoured, division was spearheaded by the tank and was the result of Germany's appreciation – after its failure in the First World War – of the importance of the tank in future warfare. Since the Treaty of Versailles forbade the use of tanks, the Germans developed their machines in secret while the Allies, fondly imagining for a while that the Germans would hold to the Treaty, failed to develop their own tanks and tactics to a parallel degree. Consequently, when the German divisions came into operation, first against Poland, in 1939, and subsequently swept through France, the Allies were taken by surprise by this swift and hard-hitting new machine. *Blitzkrieg*, or lightning war, proved devastatingly effective.

The essence of the panzer division tactic was that all the components of the division were geared to the speed of the tank. The tank was the basic weapon but a motorized arm was required to keep pace with it and to back it up. As was pointed out, a spearhead was little good without a shaft.

In conceiving tank tactics, therefore, the German army was divided into motorized and non-motorized troops. The panzer army was fully motorized. The panzer division, a unit of the panzer army, contained everything necessary for the subsistence and support of the unit.

The components of the panzer division included a reconnaissance battalion, which advanced first to scout ahead; this was followed by the main tank regiment, assisted by an engineer battalion and a regiment of panzer grenadiers to clear artificial obstacles or prepare for the crossing of such natural obstacles as rivers. The panzer artillery regiment was also used to prepare for the tank advance, while the anti-tank battalion made use of motorized anti-tank guns to clear away enemy tanks. Motor cycles, armoured troop carriers and rifle battalions were used to guard the flanks of the advancing division. Anti-aircraft guns were on hand to beat off enemy air attacks and a repair battalion was available to make running repairs on the tanks as well as the support vehicles. There were also a signal battalion and a medical staff.

Rommel, in peaked cap, watches panzer troops crossing the Mosel during the Spring offensive of 1940.

In the opening Polish campaign, there were six panzer divisions and four 'light' divisions, which later became panzer divisions. These were sufficient to break the Polish forces of 40 divisions. In the French campaign, 10 panzer divisions led the German advance, with a total strength of 2,574 tanks in the field. Although these were matched against a superior number of Allied tanks, backed up by approximately half a million more troops than the Germans put into the field, blitzkrieg tactics quickly punctured the Allied line and the panzer divisions drove deep into the heart of the enemy.

The panzer division, which initially contained nearly 400 tanks, was reduced to about half that number after the opening campaigns. Nonetheless, panzer divisions were instrumental in the rapid advance into Russia and in Rommel's desert war.

The 'PuLk' Breaks Through

The success of the panzer division against zones of resistance was largely in the tactics it employed. Initially, two waves of attack were devised. The tanks in the first wave broke through the enemy line and made for their artillery; the

second wave turned on the enemy infantry, while helping their own support through the line.

When the Russians, for one, learned to cope with this manoeuvre by closing their lines in between the two waves, another tactic, called the 'PuLk', was introduced. 'PuLk' was short for *Panzer und Lastkraftwagen*, or 'tanks and motor lorries'.

The 'PuLk' consisted of a wedge of tanks pointed at the enemy lines and protecting within its 'V' formation the supporting motorized infantry. The wedge automatically widened the gap in the enemy line created by the point so that the infantry could spill out on either side behind the enemy line. An alternative 'PuLk' was a quadrangle formation that presented a broader front and enabled the two advanced corners of the quadrangle to break off, if necessary, to form two seperate 'V' wedges.

The chief lesson learned from the panzer division was the importance of combined operations, rightly appreciated by the Germans; the chief innovation that the panzer division offered was the element of *overall* speed in attack. As a highly manoeuvrable arm, the panzer division was one of the most successful war machines.

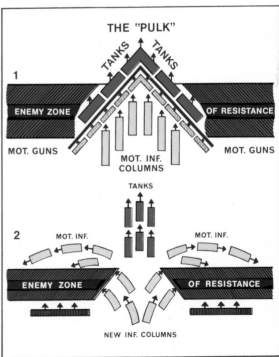

Top: German tanks in France in 1940. Men and machines were driven hard to cut off the Allies in the north.
Above: 'PuLk' formation of attack, using tanks and motorized infantry and guns.

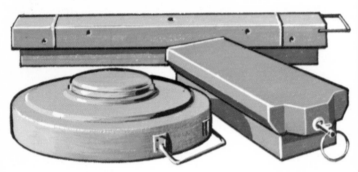

Below: The circular German Tellermine 42 and the long, thin German Riegel 43, anti-tank mines; and rectangular Italian anti-personnel mine.

MINES AND BOOBY TRAPS
The Advance of Technology

Before the invention of gunpowder the main conflict between armed forces was the clash of steel on steel, preceded occasionally by a barrage of missiles – arrows, spears, stones, whatever was available. Hand-to-hand fighting still remains an essential part of any conventional war but fire-arms have replaced the spear and the sword. For centuries battles have been decided by artillery and small arms, the confrontation of the big guns and the infantryman's rifle and, more recently, his machine gun and its variations. Tanks are fundamentally just one other way of sending a gun into action and clearing the way for other guns. But every confrontation makes use of ancillary devices, some primitive, others more sophisticated, but all of increasing importance and ingenuity with the advance of technology and its application to the battlefield.

The simple booby traps of guerilla warfare – the sharpened stake concealed in a pit and

Canadian sappers searching for mines as they enter captured Falaise, 1944.

covered with poison – lie at the bottom of the scale, though they are by no means the least effective, as the Viet Cong have shown.

The hand-grenade provided the infantryman with his own transportable bomb. With a delayed action fuse it could be made to explode at head height, if judged correctly by the thrower, and use the force of its explosion to maximum effect. Although grenades were in use in the 17th Century, probably the best known was the Mills

*Above: The detonator trips caused the German 'S' mine to explode and spread at head height.
Below: Left, Br. Shrapnel Mine Mk II; Top, Fr. light anti-tank mine, Bottom, Br. No. 75 Hawkins grenade Mk I.*

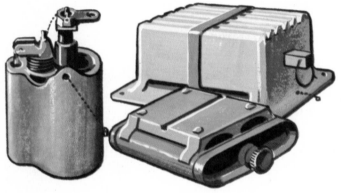

"I have expressed my deep appreciation of the well-planned and well executed work performed in so few months.

The main defence zone on the coast is strongly fortified and well manned; there are large tactical and operational reserves in the rear areas. Thousands of pieces of artillery, anti-tank guns, rocket projectiles, and flame-throwers, await the enemy; millions of mines under water and on the land lie in wait for him. In spite of the enemy's great air superiority, we can face coming events with the greatest confidence."

(signed) ROMMEL, Field Marshal   22. May 1944

These sketches of German-held beaches and defences against Allied attack were made by Field Marshall Rommel in 1944.

bomb of the Second World War, heavily relied on by the Allied infantry. Rocket-assisted grenades have been used as recently as the 1973 Middle East war.

The Minefield

Mines have proved one of the most effective devices of war. Long before the tank appeared, mines sensitive to pressure were in use, in the Crimean War and in the American Civil War. The advent of the tank established the minefield as one of the most efficient anti-tank contraptions. Mines at first designed only to disable tanks by breaking their tracks became sophisticated enough to blow up beneath their bellies and shatter the inside of the machine.

But the minefield was not restricted to tank warfare. Anti-personnel mines took a heavy toll of casualties in the Second World War and have continued to do so in subsequent conflicts.

Largely a defensive measure, mines could do the duty of a large number of soldiers in guarding a particular area and, if not preventing, then at least greatly slowing down an advance by the enemy. More sensitive than the anti-tank mine, the anti-personnel mine explodes at the contact of a foot or, like the German 'S' mine, will be thrown up into the air and explode at head height, casting a multiple charge over a wide area. More recent variations of this kind of mine are timed to explode at groin level.

Contact is no longer essential for a mine to explode. Devices sensitive to smell, sound, light and heat can be attached to mines to make them explode anywhere in the presence of humans and moving objects. In order to avoid detection by mine-sweeping devices and metal-detectors, mines can be made of plastic or wood. The mine, always insidious, has become increasingly deceptive and subtle.

BRIDGING THE GAP
Air-filled Skins

As much as the weapon itself, a war machine might be considered to be the device that assists soldiers to get to the point at which the weapon is applied – like the railway. Obstacles to the path of an armed force can be natural as well as human. Hannibal had to cross the Alps. Rivers, too, have presented serious obstacles that have had to be tackled with engineering skills and imaginative enterprise.

There are illustrations of Assyrians using air-filled bags as supports in order to help them cross rivers. These bags probably consisted of the skins of animals, sewn up and blown full of air so that they floated on the surface and provided adequate buoyancy to support a man. Many of these skins tied together could support a raft in cases where the wood itself was insufficient to sustain a heavy load – a troop of soldiers, an assault tower or battering ram, a missile-throwing machine. Hannibal himself had rivers to cross as well as mountains and used blown-up skins attached to rafts to support the weight of his elephants across the Rhône, in his advance on Rome.

A Bridge of Boats

Earlier, King Darius I of Persia had invaded Europe by means of a bridge of boats across the Bosporus. The boats were secured side by side and covered with a platform across which he brought his entire army and baggage-train. This saved him from a long and difficult journey around by land or the alternative rigours of a sea journey. He was able to overrun Thrace and Macedonia and advance north as far as the Danube. It was

Assyrian soldiers swimming to attack a city. One is using an inflated pig skin for underwater breathing.

Roman soldiers with standards shown crossing a bridge of boats, from Trajan's column.

the same Darius whose army was subsequently defeated by the Greeks at the battle of Marathon, in 490 B.C.

River crossing was generally achieved by similar, though more sophisticated, methods for the next 2,000 years. Where no adequate bridge existed, to build one of boats seemed the obvious and easiest solution. The manner in which the boats were cross-tied to each other and to the bank, the assessment and counter-action of the stresses and strains caused by the flow of the stream, these had to be taken into account; engineering such emergency bridges became a considerable science. At first constructed on the spot, when required, this was soon realized to be wasteful of time and energy when advancing troops could anticipate the need for a new crossing. Ready-prepared segments of floating bridges were engineered in advance and transported with wheels attached to their sides.

The Bailey Bridge

Floating bridges may still be used, although now the Bailey bridge, made of steel and able to span a river, is the usual equipment of engineers. This is the most famous type of bridge in use with the armed services. It was designed in 1940 by Donald Bailey and made in small sections that could easily be put together on the required site. Initially it could bear weights up to 70 tons, when several sections were joined together to traverse a river. It was used extensively by the Allies during the Second World War and still remains, in modified designs, in use today.

Right: Experiments in military bridge-building. Below right: Bailey Bridge being positioned.

THE TERROR OF FIRE
Greek Fire

Fire has probably been used, ever since it was discovered, as a means of inflicting harm to an enemy or destruction to his possessions, to burn down his dwelling or chase him out of hiding. Wooden forts and towers burned easily. Early catapults and missile-throwing devices hurled burning rags and smouldering faggots into besieged castles, whose defenders replied in like manner against the attacker's wooden engines of war with equal damage.

Ships, being also made of wood, were equally vulnerable to attack by fire, and one of the most dangerous of the early fire weapons was the famous Greek fire, which was not put out by contact with water. Greek fire would seem to have consisted, among other ingredients, of a mixture of pitch and sulphur; it created havoc and spread fear among the vessels of any enemy upon whom it was used. A burning ship at sea is one of the things most feared by any sailor. There is no way of escape, except by committing himself to the sea itself and all its dangers.

Red Hot Cannon Balls

The invention of gunpowder and the use of its explosive properties rapidly furthered the use of fire as a weapon of total destruction. Gunpowder was often used as an explosive device in its own right. Cannon balls were sometimes made red-hot before firing in the hope that they would set fire to enemy fortifications or ships or, if possible, explode the enemy's gunpowder store. It was a tricky operation to fire a red-hot cannon ball, in case it set fire to the gunpowder prematurely. Wadding was placed between the ball and the powder, and the ball had to be fired almost immediately it was put – by tongs – into the barrel.

Fire-carrying Animals

The Chinese used flaming arrows and so did many Western countries. The Mongols used live missiles: they strapped firebrands to the backs of cats and let them run among the enemy. They also used dogs and pigeons. This worked very well sometimes but more often than not, crazed by fear, the animals were as likely to run back into their own ranks as into those of the enemy. In its cruelty, this epitomized the use of fire in warfare.

Flame-throwers and Napalm

Flame-throwers came into use in the First World War. They served several purposes. At close range they were an effective way of clearing out an enemy trench or pill box, where the contents of the entrenchment could not be clearly seen and it was necessary to make certain of maximum coverage and destruction. The knowledge of their use might also intimidate an enemy into early surrender. Or they could be used to clear away covering foliage so that a clear field of fire could be obtained for the guns and rifles that followed. In street fighting, they were particularly useful for clearing out houses.

The French used petrol spray in 1914 and the Germans designed a gun that produced a jet of flaming oil. But the range of this was limited to 20–30 yards and the machine was too heavy to carry with any ease.

In the Second World War, flame was used more extensively, by tanks as well as infantry. The most lethal device was gelled petroleum. The Americans called it napalm and it was widely used in Korea and Vietnam with horrifying results, particularly when dropped in blanket coverage from the air. The vision of people, whether civilian or in uniform, being burned alive has an emotive impact that goes back a long way before the Spanish Inquisition and the *auto-da-fé*. The flame-thrower may have proved an ideal machine for the jungles of Burma and the foxholes of the Japanese islands but was certainly one of the most distasteful.

An arrow with flaming cloths being fired from a 17th-Century gun.

Right: Germans attack Russian fort with flame-thrower

BIOLOGICAL AND CHEMICAL WARFARE
Sulphur Fumes at Constantinople

Gas is clearly not a machine as such but as an adjunct to a military force it can make that force itself more effective. Biological and chemical warfare has been used for longer than might be imagined. Sulphur fumes were used by Mahomet at the siege of Constantinople, in 1453, and their use was contemplated – but rejected as inhuman – in the Crimean War in the middle of the 19th Century, a particularly wasteful war.

Earlier than the use of gas was the far more effective use of putrescent bodies and excretia as missiles for the ballista. Hurled into besieged fortifications, these could quickly spread disease among the confined defenders; often, they might be the bodies of their own comrades, killed outside the wall or fallen from the top of the parapets. As ever, the defenders replied in like kind, firing back similar missiles into the midst of the attacker's encampment, where disease – and famine if, in a strange country, their supplies were inadequate – often prevailed to as great a degree as in the city itself.

This was not only a medieval ploy. The cruel religious wars of the 15th Century – wars backed by religious idealism always seem to be the most cruel – among which John Zizka shone out like a guiding demon, reverted to a similar tactic at a time when death by plague was greatly feared. Such warfare was never a common resort but occurred often enough to arouse the indignation of those who knew about it and instigated a variety of codes of war that deplored such conduct. As was quickly discovered in the First World War, they deplored it to little effect.

Gas in the Trenches

Images of lines of soldiers, blindfolded, dragging their feet, with a hand resting forward on the shoulder of the man in front are easily conjured from the First World War. But although at first the use of gas incapacitated a relatively large number of soldiers, few of that number died – though many might have wished to – and there were a great deal fewer casualties once countermeasures had been learnt.

In the winter of 1914–15 the Germans attempted

French troops prepared for gas attack in First World War

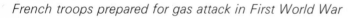

to use irritant tear gas but with poor results. Then they produced the far more lethal poisonous chlorine gas and, in 1917, liquid mustard gas. It was the initial surprise of these gases that produced the high number of early casualties and instilled emotional fear of them into the troops. But when gas masks became regulation issue and the soldiers learnt how to protect themselves against the new danger, the force of the new weapon subsided considerably.

It had, of course, its own disadvantages and dangers. More than once, like the war elephant and the firebrand animal, it turned on its own users. The wind could change suddenly or be misjudged; the gas might not clear from an enemy position before an attack was launched; cannisters of gas, like unexploded grenades, might be thrown back – there were many hazards. But the potential of this style of warfare was well realized and it was the knowledge of the very real tragedies it could bring about that prevented its use during the Second World War. Like the nuclear bomb today, the use of chemical warfare carried with it the reciprocal threat of heavy retaliation.

Nerve gases were the killers whose use everyone feared and still fears today, though they have never yet been used. The Germans stockpiled enough nerve gas during the Second World War to wipe out the population of nearly 30 main European cities.

Isolated incidents of the use of liquid gas, however, still occur in local wars, though only rarely. Tear gas of a mild kind – although victims might not agree with the adjective – is frequently used in civil disturbances.

It is a common fear that mind-affecting drugs may be infiltrated by one nation among the civilian and military population of an enemy, with damaging effects on the morale and mental stamina of that enemy. Indeed, it is supposed that such methods have, in specialized cases, already been attempted. No ban will stop such warfare so long as it proves effective and gives the warring nation yet another device with which to press its attack.

Under gas attack in First World War

Improvised gas alarm in the trenches

MISSILES ON TARGET
The Psychological Effect

The essence of a rocket, in contrast to a projectile fired from a conventional gun, is that it contains its own propellant. The advantage of this is that the rocket therefore requires a relatively simple launching platform and is, in comparison to the gun, a cheaper and more convenient method of laying down a fairly heavy barrage of fire. Its disadvantage initially – until efficient methods of guiding it to its target were discovered – lay in its inaccuracy.

It is said that the Chinese used rockets long before the Arabs are supposed to have used them in the 13th Century. But that argument is part of the larger argument about the discovery of gunpowder. Rockets were certainly used in India at the end of the 18th Century and by an Englishman, William Congreve, at the beginning of the 19th Century, after which they were used occasionally but never with any great effect beyond that of causing fear among the enemy.

The German V-weapons

The Germans became interested in rockets between the World Wars. Their experiments reached their peak with the development of the V-1 and V-2 rockets, which they turned with devastating effect on London and other British cities. These rockets seem to fall more readily into the field of aerial warfare. Closer to land, the Germans used rockets as alternatives to heavy artillery, although the rockets were never as accurate. The German *Nebelwerfer* had a range of over four miles. The Soviet multiple Katyusha rockets – usually in sets of 16, carried on the back of a lorry – had a range of about three and a half miles. The British also used rockets as extensions of mortar fire, with increased range.

Atomic Warheads

With the arrival of atomic warfare – a type of warfare that has taken its place on land, at sea and in the air and, in doing so, has dominated, with the threat it poses if not with actual use, all present and future war – the rocket has been turned to effective use as the carrier of atomic warheads. The U.S. Honest John, which originally had a range of just over 22 miles, is probably the best known of this type of rocket.

Other types followed when accurate guidance methods were discovered, such as the thin communication wire that unravelled as the rocket proceeded on its flight, or infra-red tracking devices and photographic tracking techniques. The small atomic warhead that these rockets carry, while providing a lethal and not-to-be-underestimated punch, will inflict only limited damage, the effects of which can be estimated in a way that the megaton explosion of a full-size atomic device never can be. The ostensible limitations of the field of effect of such rocket missiles is dangerous if it encourages nations to think that they can get away with using them without reprisals; although total war might be sidestepped, nervous tension would greatly increase to the detriment of balanced judgment. The increasing ability to pack atomic warheads into yet smaller and smaller containers, so that they can easily be transported across national borders, must be viewed with considerable alarm.

Left: Rocket practice on the marshes, 1845, by the Royal Artillery.

Right: Russian-made SAM missiles on the way back to Israel to be examined by their captors.

Above: Releasing carrier pigeon from tank, 1918.
Below: Carrier pigeon cages on donkey cart.

COMMUNICATIONS AND COMPUTERS

Good communications are important on the battlefield. Without them, coordination of movement is virtually impossible, messages become garbled, confusion is inevitable and the movement of troops greatly hindered. Communication between the battlefield and the source of command, which may well be many miles away, is equally important.

The Romans built a thorough system of roads to enable good communications between the capital and the distant frontiers of the Empire. Cyrus of Persia established a messenger service throughout his empire; it consisted of a carefully planned system of post houses and horses that enabled a messenger to travel 1,600 miles in a week. The vast Mongol Empire also used fast horseback links between its outlying districts and its centre.

Written words ensured greater accuracy than the spoken message, though the former could often be intercepted by the enemy. Bonfires set on hilltops and established in a series over a great distance could transmit pre-arranged signals. The use of modern semaphore, invented by John Edgeworth, a racehorse owner, in 1767, was taken up by France in the Napoleonic Wars in a

Bottom left: Signal post for battery.
Below: Tandem bicycle frame
used by Germans to generate
electricity for wireless in the trenches.
Far right: Signal station
using daylight lamps
at the Battle of Arras, 1917.

chain of relay-stations to keep Paris informed of the activities of her armies at the frontiers.

Each technological advance in communications during the 19th Century was used to great advantage on the battlefield. The electric telegraph, first set up in 1838, the first use of Morse code in 1844, Alexander Graham Bell's telephone of 1876, the invention of the radio at the turn of the century – these were all adopted by the military as machines to use in war. Immediate communication between headquarters and the front line, telephonic range-guidance from forward posts to heavy artillery, co-ordination of advance between troops miles apart, these were only some of the diverse applications of the new technology.

The watch, made accurate and compact toward the end of the 17th Century, was one of the most important devices that contributed toward more precise co-ordination of movement. Combined assaults could be timed exactly without resort to the give-away visual communication, carried message or pre-arranged signal, all of which were either vulnerable to interception or liable to fatal inaccuracy.

Satellite communication systems now allow long-range telephone conversations that have, for instance, enabled the President of the United States to communicate orders directly to his generals in Vietnam or to keep in constant touch with his Secretary of State in the Middle East. Satellites are also used by the superpowers to keep a watchful eye on each other's military installations.

Computers with Memories

Information gained from satellites, information fed in from observation posts in the field, information pre-gathered on enemy statistics – all this can be fed into computers to provide an instant analysis of strategic and tactical situations, minimizing the time-lag necessary for a decision on the right course of action. The memory-stored computer is the latest brain at the head of the communications network that forms the nervous system of the modern army. Automation in this field, as in every other, continues to proceed at an astonishing rate. Only a century or so divides the smoke-signal from the satellite. What might follow in this line constitutes one of the most fascinating fields of military study.

PSYCHOLOGICAL WARFARE
The Printing Press Goes to War

The history of psychological warfare goes back to ancient times. The bluff and counter-bluff of the war of nerves, the stirring of fear, the undermining of confidence, the play on human susceptibility – all are tricks as old as the history of human conflict

Psychological warfare used *against* enemy troops and civilians must be distinguished from propaganda on the home front – encouraging the morale of the nation. Both weapons – offensive and defensive – have an equally long history and are equally important in this style of warfare.

The invention of printing in Western Europe in the middle of the 15th Century added yet another machine to the armoury of warfare, a machine as valuable as the hardest hitting weapon. Ideas on the art and science of waging war could be disseminated with much greater ease and to a far wider range of public by means of the printed word, from Macchiavelli's *The Prince* and *The Art of War* to the writings of Maurice de Saxe, Frederick the Great, Clausewitz and such modern military thinkers as Liddell-Hart, J. F. C. Fuller and even T. E. Lawrence, whose *Pillars of Wisdom* was a brilliant assessment of the function of guerilla warfare as well as a philosophical work of great depth and learning.

Printing also furthered the dissemination of ideas associated with incentives to war on the home front, instigations such as the religious tracts and diatribes of, for instance, the 17th Century, leaflets, newspapers, information that was sometimes (rarely) truth, sometimes half-

Above: First World War poster, in which Lord Kitchener exhorted his countrymen to enlist.
Right: American wartime poster to encourage home grown produce.
Far Right: American recruiting poster of the First World War: an alarmist image.

Left: A 17th-Century satire on the Puritans from a set of Cavalier playing cards.

DESTROY THIS MAD BRUTE
ENLIST
U.S. ARMY

truth but always acceptable to the mass of the public because it bore the status of the printed word – a stamp that impressed too many.

The speed with which the printed word spread information meant that people's sympathies for, and antagonisms against, any military action could be quickly aroused. First by the printed word, later by radio, today by television as well, events on the battlefront are reported within hours, often within minutes of their occurrence – reported not only to those who must make the decisions but also to the public upon whose mood at times the political decision must rely for support. Between the event and the reporting of the event, there is always room for the slight alteration that will shift the attitude of the listener.

Slogans and Incentives

Propaganda is concerned with, as the word implies, the propagation of ideas. It has been common practice for nations at war to use propaganda posters both to incense the population against the enemy and to call the people to arms. 'Your Country Needs You' has been a popular

theme spelled out in a variety of ways by many countries over the centuries. It is some measure of the appeal of this kind of propaganda and to the care with which it was produced that many of these posters have become eagerly sought collectors' items.

Another common practice has been to drop leaflets over enemy territory in the hope that the population, civilian as well as military, may either be subverted into the enemy camp or persuaded of the futility of resistance and the advisability of laying down their arms. This practice has continued to find favour in the communist wars of recent years in Asia.

During the Second World War, the Germans became experts at propaganda, though modern research shows that the Allies were as least as active and probably more successful in this field. Goebbels' slogans spread like wildfire: 'The Germans are a super race destined to rule the world', 'Today Germany, tomorrow the world'. While the Japanese aroused their soldiers to 'Smash the red-haired barbarians of the West', their leaflets attempted with absurd over-

Wartime poster asking for civilian help

emphasis to set the G.I.s against the prospect of fighting: a pretty girl says, 'Don't want to die. Before the bombs fall let me take your hand and kiss your gentle cheeks and murmur. Before the terror comes let me walk beside you in the garden deep in petalled sleep. Let me, while there is still time and place. Feel soft against me and rest your warm hand on my breast.'

Radio programmes of a similar nature were also put out both by the Germans and Japanese on wavelengths that the Allies would pick up. One of the most famous of these was the voice of Lord Haw-Haw (an Englishman named William Joyce) whose admonitions to Londoners were easily picked up on home radios.

Propaganda is as insidious as advertising and, in its most sophisticated forms, a good deal more difficult to assess as truth or falsehood. It plays on uncertainty and doubt, fundamental beliefs, the gullibility, the pride, the hopes, fears and weaknesses of human nature. Of all the devices of war, it is the one which we can least understand, the one that we cannot counter, except by remaining constantly vigilant, in war and peace.

German poster exhorting defence of family and land

Above: Distributing propaganda leaflets by balloon.
Below: Propaganda photograph of chivalrous German giving wounded British soldier the last of his Brandy.

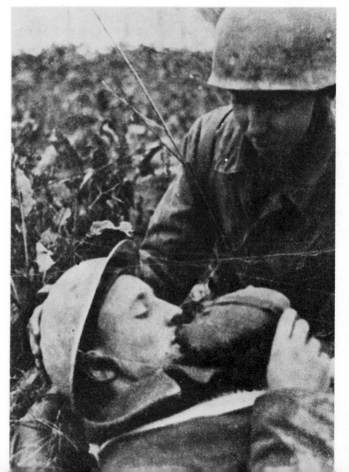

INDEX

ACKNOWLEDGEMENTS

The publishers would like to thank the following organisations and individuals for their kind permission to reproduce the pictures in this book:

Aerofilms 26/27

American History Picture Library 82, 82/83 (Smithsonian Institution), 84 centre right and bottom right, 91 (Imperial War Museum), 92/93, 104 centre right (Vickers), 116

British Tourist Authority 20 bottom left

Camera Press 127, 131

J. Allen Cash 21

Crown Copyright/Permission of the Controller H.M.S.O. back cover, 60 centre and bottom, 78/79 centre, bottom left and bottom right, 79 centre and bottom right, 80 top and bottom, 87 top

Mary Evans Picture Library 36/37 top, 44, 58, 61, 73 top, 76 bottom left, 78, 88/89, 100 top left, 125 centre, 126, 134

Expression Photo Library front cover

Sonia Halliday Photographs 17 top, 32, 55 top and centre

Michael Holford 10/11, 11 top and bottom, 14/15, 18/19, 22/23, 38, 41, 42/43, 52, 54/55, 59, 124, 130, 135

Robert Hunt Library 93 top (Imperial War Museum), 97 top and centre left, 106/107, 112/113, 118/119 centre (Imperial War Museum), 120/121 (Bundesarchive), 121 top right, 122 centre right (Associated Press), 123 top right

Imperial War Museum 89, 93 bottom, 100 top right, 101 top left and top right, 104 top right, 104/105, 105 centre left and bottom left, 108 centre and bottom left, 108/109, 113, 114, 117, 118/119 bottom, 119 centre and bottom right, 125 bottom right, 128/129, 129, 132 top left, centre left and bottom left, 132/133, 133, 134/135 centre top and centre bottom, 136, 137 top right, bottom left and bottom right

Luxembourg Embassy 73 bottom

Mansell Collection 16, 34/35, 36/37 bottom, 40, 45, 48, 64, 64/65, 65, 66/67, 76 top, 76/77, 77, 124/125

National Gallery, London 50/51

Novosti Press Agency 57 top, 104 bottom right

RAC Tank Museum 101 centre right

Radio Times Hulton Picture Library 72, 116/117

Ronan Picture Library 17 bottom, 32/33, 48/49, 68

Spectrum 2/3 and 142/143, 6/7, 53, 56/57

Wadsworth Atheneum, Hartford, Conn. 84 top right

Weidenfeld Archiv 74/75 (Waffensammlung des Kunsthistorischen Museums, Vienna), 81 (Bildarchiv der österreichescen Nationalbibliothek, Vienna)

Derrick E. Witty 84 centre and bottom left, 85 centre left, bottom left and bottom right, 86/87, 87 bottom, 88
Illustrations by Hildergarde Bone, Wilf Hardy, Peter Jackson, Bill Robertshaw